THE
ZOO
JOKE
BOOK

500 Rude Jokes and Cartoons

Text and illustrations copyright © 2005 Emap Consumer Media
Design copyright © 2005 Carlton Books Limited

This edition published by Carlton Books Limited 2005
20 Mortimer Street
London W1T 3JW

A CIP catalogue record for this book is available from the
British Library.

ISBN-10: 1-86200-230-4
ISBN-13: 978-1-86200-230-2

Printed in Great Britain
Typeset by the friendly guys at e-type, Liverpool

THE ZOO JOKE BOOK

500 Rude Jokes and Cartoons

SevenOaks

Contents

SEX

ACUTE ANGINA

An elderly couple go to bed together for the first time.

The old woman says, 'Before we start, I have to warn you that I have acute angina.'

The old man looks her up and down and says, 'Yes, and your tits aren't bad either.'

AIDS

A man and a woman are having sex.

The woman says, 'You haven't got AIDS, have you?'

He says no.

She says, 'Thank God. I don't want to catch that again.'

ANGELS

A girl is standing at the gates of heaven when she hears screams of pain coming from inside.

She says to St Peter, 'What's going on?'

He says, 'That's the sound of new angels getting big holes drilled into their backs for their wings, and small holes drilled into their heads for their halos.'

She says, 'Heaven sounds terrible. I think I'd rather go to hell.'

St Peter says, 'In hell, you'll be constantly raped and sodomised.'

She says, 'That's OK, I've already got holes for that.'

AUSTRALIAN KISS

Q. What's an Australian kiss?

A. The same as a French kiss, but Down Under.

BITE YOUR BREASTS

A bloke walking down the street sees a woman with perfect breasts.

He says, 'Hey, would you let me bite your breasts for £100?'

She says, 'Are you mad?'

He says, 'OK, would you let me bite your breasts for £1,000?'

She says, 'I'm not that kind of woman! Got it?'

He says, 'OK, would you let me bite your breasts just once for £10,000?'

She thinks about it and says, 'OK, just once, but not here. Let's go to that dark alley over there.'

So they go into the alley, where she takes off her blouse to reveal the most perfect breasts in the world.

As soon as he sees them, he grabs them and starts caressing them, fondling them slowly, kissing them, licking them, burying his face in them – but not biting them.

The woman eventually gets annoyed and says, 'Well? Are you going to bite them or not?'

'Nah,' he says. 'Costs too much.'

BONDAGE-LOVING SON

A mother is cleaning her 12-year-old son's bedroom when she finds a series of bondage and fetish mags.

She shouts for her husband to come and see.

She yells, 'What the hell am I supposed to do about this lot?'

The father says, 'I don't know, but whatever you do, don't spank him.'

BOY'S BRAINS

A three-year-old boy is examining his testicles in the bath.

'Mum,' he says, 'are these my brains?'

His mother says, 'Not yet.'

BRIDGE

Q. How is the card game Bridge like sex?

A. If you don't have a good partner, you'd better have a good hand.

BULL

Q. What does a bull do to stay warm on a cold day?
A. He slips into a nice warm Jersey.

BUNGEE JUMPS AND OLD LADIES

Q. What have a bungee jump and a blow-job from an 80-year-old got in common?
A. They're great if you don't look down.

BUNGEE JUMPS AND PROSTITUTES

Q. What do a bungee jump and a prostitute have in common?
A. They're cheap, fast and if the rubber breaks, you're dead.

CHEAP PUB

A man in a pub asks for a pint.

The barman says, 'Sure, that'll be a penny.'

'A penny?' exclaims the man. Reading the menu, he says, 'Could I have steak and chips?'

'Certainly,' says the barman, 'that'll be fourpence.'

'Four pence?' cries the man. 'You're joking. Where's the bloke who owns this place?'

The barman says, 'Upstairs, with my wife.'

The man says, 'What's he doing upstairs with your wife?'

The barman says, 'The same thing I'm doing to his business.'

CHEATING WIFE

A cheating wife is having sex with her lover when the phone rings. She picks it up, listens for a couple of minutes, puts it down and says, 'That was my husband.'

Worried, her lover starts to put his clothes on.

'Calm down,' she says, 'we've got plenty of time. He's playing cards with you and the rest of his mates.'

CHINESE WOMAN

A guy goes to a disco, picks up a Chinese woman and takes her home.

She says, 'I'll do anything you want.'

He says, 'How about a 69?'

She says, 'I'm not cooking at this time of night.'

CINDERELLA

Q. What did Cinderella do when she got to the ball?
A. Gag.

CLOSED EYES

Q. Why do women close their eyes during sex?
A. Because they can't stand to see a man having a good time.

COLD HANDS

Two lovers go to the mountains for a winter break and the man goes out to chop wood.

When he gets back, he says to his girlfriend, 'My hands are freezing.'

She says, 'Well, put them between my legs to warm up.'

He does, and it works.

After lunch, he goes back out to chop more wood, comes back and says again, 'My hands are freezing.'

Again she says, 'Put them between my legs.'

He does, and again it works.

After dinner, he goes to chop wood for the night. When he returns, he says, 'Darling, my hands are freezing!'

She looks at him and says, 'For crying out loud, don't your ears ever get cold?'

'Can't you give the dummy mouth-to-mouth without getting romantically involved, Mrs Wilks?'

CONFESSIONS

A virgin couple are on their honeymoon.

Before they have sex, the wife says she has something to confess.

The husband says, 'I will love you no matter what it is. Tell me.'

The wife tells him that she is extremely flat-chested.

The husband takes off her shirt and says, 'Yes, you're small, but I love you anyway. Now, I have something to confess too.'

She says, 'I will love you no matter what it is. Tell me.'

He says, 'OK. I'm built like a baby down there.'

She says, 'I can deal with that.'

So he pulls down his pants and his wife passes out. He fans her and she finally gets up.

She says, 'I thought you said you were built like a baby?'

He says, 'Yes: 7lbs, 21 inches.'

DARK FOREST

A couple start having sex in the middle of a dark forest.

After about 15 minutes, the man gets up and says, 'Damn, I wish I had a torch.'

The woman says, 'Me too – you've been eating grass for the last 10 minutes.'

DEAD WIFE

Q. How can you tell if your wife is dead?
A. The sex is the same, but the dishes pile up.

DEAF COUPLE

A deaf couple are in bed and, because they can't sign in the dark, they need to find a way to tell each other they want sex.

So the next day the man signs to the woman, 'If I want sex,

I'll squeeze your boob once. If not, I'll squeeze it twice. If you want sex, pull my cock once. If not, pull it 100 times.'

DOCTOR'S SEX HELP

A doctor has a great reputation for helping couples improve their sex life, but always promises not to take a case if he feels he can't help them.

The Browns come to see the doctor, and he gives them thorough physical examinations. He concludes, 'Yes, I'm happy to say that I can help you. On your way home from my surgery, stop at the supermarket and buy some grapes and some doughnuts. Go home, take off your clothes, and you, sir, roll the grapes across the floor until you make a bullseye in your wife's crotch. Then, on hands and knees, you must crawl to her like a leopard and retrieve the grape using only your tongue.'

He adds, 'Ma'am, you must take the doughnuts and, from across the room, toss them at your husband until you make a ringer around his penis. Then, like a lioness, you must crawl to him and eat the doughnut, using only your lips.'

The couple go home and their sex life becomes more and more wonderful.

They tell their friends, the Greens, that they should see the doctor.

The doctor tells the Greens he won't take the case unless he feels he can help them. So he conducts the same physical examinations.

Then he tells the Greens the bad news. 'I can't help you. I believe your sex life is as good as it will ever be.'

The Greens plead with him, and say, 'You helped our friends the Browns; now please help us.'

The doctor says, 'Oh, all right. On your way home, stop at the supermarket and buy some apples and a box of Cheerios...'

DOUBLE ENTENDRE

A woman walks into a pub and asks for a double entendre.
So the landlord gives her one.

'Don't worry, when he starts downloading porn it just means he's hungry.'

DOGGY STYLE

A woman tells her doctor that she's got bad carpet burns on her knees.

The doctor asks how she got them and she tells him it's from having sex doggy-style.

The doctor bandages her knees.

She says, 'What can I do to avoid this?'

He says, 'Couldn't you try having sex in different positions?'

She says, 'That's OK for me, but what about the dog?'

DUCK AND PIG

A man comes home one night from the pub with a duck under his arm. He says, 'This is the pig I've been shagging.'

His wife says, 'That's a duck.'
He says, 'I was talking to the duck.'

DYING MAN

A bloke gets back from the doctor's one day and tells his wife he's only got 24 hours to live.

Wiping away her tears, he asks her to have sex with him. Of course, she agrees, and they make passionate love.

Six hours later, he says, 'Darling, now I have only 18 hours to live. Can we have sex again?'

She agrees.

Later, he's getting into bed when he realises he now has only eight hours of life left.

He says, 'Darling? Please? Just one more time before I die.'

She agrees; then afterwards she rolls over and falls asleep.

He, however, hears the clock ticking, and he tosses and turns until he's down to only four more hours. He taps his wife on the shoulder to wake her up.

He says, 'Darling, I only have four hours left. Could we...?'

His wife sits up abruptly and yells, 'Look, I have to get up in the morning - you don't.'

EGG

What are the three worst things about being an egg?

You only get laid once, it takes ten minutes to go hard and the only bird to sit on your face is your mum.

EXPLODING BOILER

Q. What do you do if your boiler explodes?
A. Buy her some flowers.

Eggs and Money

A woman on her death bed calls her husband and instructs him to look under their bed and open the wooden box he finds.

He's puzzled by the three eggs and £7,000 in cash he finds inside, so he asks his wife what the eggs are for.

'Oh, those?' she says. 'Every time we had bad sex, I put an egg in the box.'

Not bad after 35 years of marriage, thinks the husband.

Then he says, 'But what about the £7,000?'

'Oh, that?' she says. 'Every time I got a dozen I sold them.'

FAKE ORGASMS

Q. Why do woman fake orgasms?
A. Because they think men care.

FAT-FINGERED LESBIAN

Q. What do you call a lesbian with fat fingers?
A. Well-endowed.

FAT WOMEN AND MOPEDS

Q. What have a fat woman and a moped got in common?
A. They're both OK for a ride until your mates find out.

IN CAR ENTERTAINMENT
LEATHER UPHOLSTERY
TWIN AIR-BAGS

FEMALE SPERM

Q. Why is it that it's mainly female sperm that find the egg first?
A. Male sperm won't stop and ask for directions.

GAY SEX INTERRUPTED

Two gay men are having sex when the phone starts to ring.

One of them rises to answer it and says, 'I'll be just a minute. Don't finish yourself off until I get back.'

The second bloke says, 'OK.'

A few minutes later, the first bloke comes back into the room and sees semen everywhere.

The first bloke says, 'I told you to wait till I got back before you finished.'

The second bloke says, 'I didn't; I just farted.'

HARD TO SOFT

Q. What goes in hard and pink, but comes out soft and mushy?
A. Bubblegum.

HEADACHE CURE

A bloke is suffering from severe headaches.

The doctor says, 'I suffered from that type of headache for years, too. This is how I cured it. Every day I'd give my wife oral sex. When she came, she'd squeeze her legs together with all her strength, and the pressure would relieve the tension in my head. Try that every day for two weeks, then come back and let me know how it goes.'

Two weeks go by and the man is back.

He says, 'Doctor, I feel great. I haven't had a headache since I started this treatment. I can't thank you enough.'

The doctor says, 'Glad to hear it.'

The man says, 'Thanks. And by the way, you have a lovely home.'

HEAD NURSE

Q. How can you tell who's the head nurse?
A. She's the one with the dirty knees.

HEART SURGEON'S FUNERAL

A heart surgeon dies and is given an elaborate funeral.

An enormous heart covered in flowers stands behind the casket during the service.

Following the eulogy, the heart opens, and the casket rolls inside.

The heart then closes, sealing the surgeon inside the beautiful heart for ever.

At that point, one of the mourners bursts into laughter. Everyone stares at him.

He says, 'I'm sorry; I was just thinking of my own funeral. I'm a gynaecologist.'

That's when the rectal surgeon fainted.

HOLES

Q. Why do women have two holes so close together?
A. In case you miss.

JELLY BABY

A jelly baby goes to the doctor and asks if he can have an AIDS test.

The doctor says, 'Why? What the hell have you been up to?'

The jelly baby says, 'Fucking allsorts.'

"Smirking or Non-Smirking ?"

KINKY GERMAN

A German visits a prostitute and says, 'I vish to buy sex vit you. I must varn you: I am a little kinky.'

The prostitute says, 'No problem.'

So off they go to the prostitute's flat, where the German produces four large bedsprings and a duck call.

He says, 'I vant you to tie ze springs to each of your limbs.'

The prostitute finds this odd, but complies, fastening the springs to her hands and knees.

He says, 'Now you vill get on your hans und knees.'

She obeys, balancing on the springs.

He says, 'You vill please blow zis vistle as I make love to you.'

She thinks this weird but it seems harmless and after all, the German is paying.

The sex is fantastic. She is bounced all over the room by the energetic German, all the time honking on the duck call.

The climax is the most sensational that she has ever

experienced, and it's several minutes before she's recovered her breath sufficiently to say, 'That was amazing. What do you call that?'

The German says, 'Four sprung duck technique.'

KY JELLY

A man goes into a chemist and asks if they've got any KY jelly.

The woman behind the counter says, 'Sorry, we haven't. Have you tried Boots?'

The man says, 'I want to slide in, not march in.'

LEPER AND PROSTITUTE

Q. What did the leper say to the prostitute?
A. 'Keep the tip.'

LITTLE GIRL AND SANTA

A little girl goes to see Santa.

Santa says, 'What would you like Santa to bring you for Christmas?'

She says, 'I want a Barbie and Action Man.'

Santa says, 'I thought Barbie came with Ken.'

She says, 'No: she comes with Action Man; she fakes it with Ken.'

LOUD IN BED

A woman goes to her therapist and moans, 'Every time we're in bed and my husband has an orgasm, he lets out an ear-splitting yell.'

The therapist says, 'That's completely natural. I don't see what the problem is.'

She says, 'It wakes me up.'

LOVE AND HERPES

Q. What's the difference between love and herpes?
A. Love doesn't last for ever.

MACS AND NUNS

Q. What do you get if you cross a Mac with a nun?
A. A computer that will never go down on you.

MAD OLD LADY

Ethel is a demon in her wheelchair, and loves to charge around the nursing home, taking corners on one wheel and getting up to maximum speed on the long corridors.

Because the poor woman is one sandwich short of a picnic, the other residents tolerate her, and some of the blokes even join in.

One day, Ethel is speeding up the corridor when a door opens and Mad Clarence steps forward with his arm outstretched.

'Stop!' he shouts. 'Have you got a licence for that thing?'

Ethel fishes around in her handbag, pulls out a Kit Kat wrapper and holds it up to him.

'OK,' he says, and Ethel speeds off down the hall.

As she takes the corner near the TV lounge on one wheel, Weird Harold pops out in front of her and shouts, 'Stop! Have you got proof of insurance?'

Ethel digs into her handbag, pulls out a beermat and holds it up to him.

Harold nods and says, 'Carry on, ma'am.'

As Ethel nears the final corridor before the front door, Crazy Craig steps out in front of her, stark naked, with a huge erection in his hand.

'Oh, good grief,' says Ethel, 'not the breathalyser again.'

MAFIA AND CUNNILINGUS

Q. What do the Mafia and cunnilingus have in common?
A. One slip of the tongue and you're in deep shit.

MARTIAN SWINGERS

The year is 2222 and Mike and Maureen land on Mars after accumulating enough frequent flier miles.

They meet a Martian couple and have a chat. Maureen brings up the subject of sex.

She says, 'Just how do you guys do it?'

The Martian says, 'Pretty much the way you do.'

The couples decide to swap partners for the night to see what it's like.

Maureen and the male Martian go off to a bedroom where the Martian strips. He's got a tiny penis - half an inch long and a quarter of an inch thick.

Maureen says, 'I don't think this is going to work. It's just not long enough.'

The Martian says, 'No problem', and proceeds to slap his forehead with his palm. With each slap of his forehead, his penis grows until it's impressively long.

She says, 'That's great, but it's still pretty thin.'

The Martian says, 'No problem', and starts pulling his ears. With each pull, his penis grows thicker and thicker until it's huge.

'Wow!' she says, as they fall into bed and have passionate sex.

The next day the couples rejoin their normal partners and go their separate ways.

Mike says, 'Well, was it any good?'

Maureen says, 'I hate to say it, but it was wonderful. How about you?'

He says, 'It was horrible. All I got was a headache - she kept slapping my forehead and pulling my ears.'

MASTURBATION PROBLEM

A bloke goes to his optometrist to have his eyes examined.
   The optometrist says, 'Joe, you've got to stop masturbating!'
   Joe says, 'Why, Doc? Am I going blind?'
   The optometrist says, 'No, but you're upsetting my other patients.'

MICE

Q. How many mice does it take to screw in a light-bulb?
A. Two, if they're small enough.

MISS PIGGY

Q. Why can't Miss Piggy count to 70?
A. She gets a frog in her throat at 69.

Naked Fare

One rainy night, a taxi driver spots an arm waving from the shadows of an alley.

Even before he rolls to a stop at the kerb, a figure leaps into the cab and slams the door. Checking his mirror as he pulls away, the cabbie is startled to see a dripping wet, naked woman sitting in the back seat.

'Er... where to?' he stammers.

'The station,' says the woman.

'OK,' he says, taking another long glance in the mirror.

The woman catches him staring and says, 'What are you looking at, driver?'

The driver says, 'Well, I'd noticed you're completely naked and was wondering how you'll pay your fare.'

Nodding slowly, the woman spreads her legs and puts her feet up on the back of the front seat.

She smiles at the driver and says, 'Does that answer your question?'

'Bloody hell,' cries the cabbie. 'Got anything smaller?'

NAKED WIFE

A man and his wife go on a second honeymoon for their 25th anniversary.

At the hotel, the woman says, 'When you first saw my naked body, what was going through your mind?'

The man says, 'All I wanted to do was to fuck your brains out and suck your tits dry.'

Then, as the wife seductively undresses, she says, 'What are you thinking now?'

He says, 'It looks as if I did a pretty good job.'

NUNS IN THE BATH

Two nuns are in the bath.

One nun says to the other, 'Where's the soap?'

The other says, 'Yes, it does, doesn't it?'

NYMPHO PARROT

Did you hear about the nymphomaniac parrot?

She liked a cock or two.

OLD MEN'S SEX LIVES

Two old men are comparing their libidos.

The first one says, 'I can still do it twice.'

The other says, 'Which time do you prefer?'

The first one says, 'Usually the winter.'

ORAL AND ANAL

Q. What's the difference between oral sex and anal sex?

A. Oral sex makes your day, anal sex makes your hole weak.

OLYMPIC CONDOMS

A man is out shopping and discovers a new brand of condoms – Olympic.

He buys a pack, then tells his wife.

She says, 'Olympic condoms? What makes them so special?'

He says, 'There are three colours: gold, silver and bronze.'

She says, 'What colour are you going to wear tonight?'

He says, 'Gold, of course!'

She says, 'Can't you wear silver? It would be nice if you didn't come first for once.'

PAPER BAG

A paper bag goes to the doctors and says, 'There's something wrong with my privates.'

The doctor has a look and says, 'I'm sorry to say you have AIDS.'

The paper bag says, 'How? I'm a virgin – I've never had sex.'

The doctor says, 'Your mum must be a carrier.'

PENGUIN'S ICE CREAM

A penguin's driving when all of a sudden his car breaks down.

He waddles into a garage and asks the mechanic to look at his car.

The mechanic says, 'Leave the car with us and come back in an hour.'

The penguin waddles off. On his way he sees an ice-cream van and buys an ice-cream. A messy eater, he gets the ice-cream all over his face and flippers.

On his return to the garage, the penguin says to the mechanic, 'What seems to be the problem?'

The mechanic says, 'It looks like you've blown a seal.'

The penguin says, 'No, it's only ice-cream.'

PENIS MEDICINE

A man emerges from the bathroom naked and climbs into bed in the mood for sex, but, as usual, his wife says, 'I have a headache.'

'Don't worry,' he says. 'I was just in the bathroom powdering my cock with aspirin. You can take it orally or as a suppository: it's up to you.'

PEOPLE COME APART

A young boy says, 'Mum, is it true people come apart like machines?'

She replies, 'Of course not, darling. What gave you that idea?'

The boy says, 'I overheard Daddy on the phone saying he was screwing the arse off his secretary.'

"Is this birds and bees chat going to take long? I'm late for my pre-natal class."

PERVERT DOCTOR

A girl goes to the doctor. The doctor, a pervert, tells her to strip and lie on the couch.

He starts playing with her breasts and says, 'Do you know what I'm doing?'

She says, 'Yes, you're checking my breasts for lumps.'

He starts rubbing her thigh and says, 'Do you know what I'm doing now?'

She says, 'Yes, you're checking my skin for eczema.'

Then he gets his cock out and starts having sex with her, and says, 'Do you know what I'm doing now?'

She says, 'Yes, you're contracting genital warts, which is why I came here in the first place.'

PICKLE SLICER

A bloke has a new job in a pickle factory.

For weeks, he has a strange urge to stick his dick into the pickle slicer.

He finally comes clean to his wife, who begs him not to do it.

But he can't control himself, and his urge grows greater and greater.

One day he comes home from work, and tells his wife that he's done it.

'My God!' says his wife, 'what happened?'

'I got fired,' says the bloke.

'No,' says his wife, 'I mean, what happened about the pickle slicer?'

'Oh,' says the bloke, 'she got fired too.'

PITBULL

Q. What do you get if you cross a pitbull with a prostitute?
A. Your last blow-job.

PIXIE

Q. When is a pixie not a pixie?
A. When he's got his head up a fairy's skirt – then he's a goblin.

PLAYING BONGOS

A man is lying naked on a beach when a sexy girl comes over and starts slapping his arse rhythmically.
He says, 'What are you doing?'
She says, 'Playing the bongos.'
He turns over and says, 'Can you play the flute?'

PORK PIES AND HANDJOBS

A bloke's walking down the street when he sees a sign in the window of a local shop: 'Pork pies 50p, hand-jobs £1.'
He goes in and sees the most beautiful girl behind the counter.
He says, 'Are you the girl who gives hand-jobs for a pound?'
She nods.
He says, 'Wash your hands, then; I want a pork pie.'

PREGNANCY CONFUSION

A man comes home one night, and his wife throws her arms around his neck and cries, 'Darling, I have great news: I'm a month overdue. I think we're going to have a baby! The doctor gave me a test today, but until we find out for sure, we can't tell anybody.'
The next day, a bloke from the electric company rings the doorbell, because the couple haven't paid their last bill.

He says, 'Are you Mrs Smith? You're a month overdue.'

'How did you know?' stammers the young woman.

'It's in our files,' says the man.

'What? Well, let me talk to my husband about this tonight.'

That night, she tells her husband about the visit, and he, mad as a bull, rushes to the electric company's office first thing the next morning.

He yells, 'What's going on? You have it on file that my wife is a month overdue? What business is that of yours?'

'Just calm down,' says the bloke, 'it's nothing serious. All you have to do is pay us.'

'Pay you? And if I refuse?'

'In that case, sir, we'd have no option but to cut yours off.'

'And what would my wife do then?'

'I don't know. I suppose she'd have to use a candle.'

PREGNANT NUN

Q. How do you get a nun pregnant?

A. Dress her up as an altar-boy.

PREGNANT TEEN

An 18-year-old girl tells her mother she's missed her period for two months.

Worried, the mother buys a pregnancy test kit. The result shows that the girl is pregnant.

Furious, the mother yells, 'Who was the pig that did this to you?'

The girl picks up the phone and makes a call.

Half an hour later a Ferrari stops outside.

A man in a very expensive suit climbs out and enters the house.

He sits in the living room with the father, the mother and the girl, and says, 'Your daughter has informed me of the problem. I can't marry her because of my family situation, but I'll take charge. If a girl is born, I will bequeath her two shops, a townhouse, a beach villa and a £1,000,000 bank account. If a boy is born, my legacy will be a couple of factories and a £2,000,000 bank account. If it's twins, a factory and £1,000,000 each. However, if there is a miscarriage, what do you suggest I do?'

The father places a hand firmly on the man's shoulder and says, 'Fuck her again.'

PROSTITUTE'S NOSE

Q. What do you call a prostitute with a runny nose?
A. Full.

PUBLIC SCHOOLBOY

Q. How do you know if a public schoolboy is a gentlemen?
A. He'll take a girl out five times before shagging her younger brother.

REALISTIC VIBRATOR

They've invented the most realistic vibrator yet.

Just before she orgasms, the vibrator comes, goes limp, farts and switches itself off.

REDNECK COUPLE

A married redneck couple are sitting on the couch watching the news on TV in Alabama.

The man says, 'Look at them homosexuals demanding the right to be married. They're ruining the sanctity of our institution. We oughta go to San Francisco just to show those liberals that marriage means one man, one woman. Right, darling?'

The woman says, 'Right, Daddy!'

RUBIK'S CUBES AND PENISES

Q. What do a Rubik's Cube and a penis have in common?
A. The longer you play with them, the harder they get.

SCOTTISH WOMAN

A Scottish woman walks in on her husband wanking into a welly.

She yells, 'Stop fucking aboot!'

SENSITIVE CONDOMS

Have you heard about the new super-sensitive condoms?

They hang around after the man leaves and talk to the woman.

Redundancy

Mr Smith has two employees, Sarah and Jack.

They're both extremely good workers. However, Mr Smith looks over his books one day and decides that he isn't making enough money to warrant two employees, and he'll have to make one redundant.

But he has trouble finding a fair way to do it. He decides to watch them work, and the first one to take a break will be the one he lays off.

So he sits in his office and watches them. Suddenly, Sarah gets a headache and needs to take an aspirin. She takes the aspirin out of her purse and goes to the water cooler to get a drink to wash it down.

Mr Smith follows her to the water cooler, taps her on the shoulder and says, 'Sarah, I'm going to have to lay you or Jack off.'

Sarah says, 'I have a headache – can you jack off?'

SMALL PENIS

A bloke is very ashamed because he has an extremely small penis and doesn't want his girlfriend to dump him when she sees its size.

One night when he and his girlfriend are snogging in a dark corner he decides to show her. The man unzips his trousers, whips out his tiny penis and shoves it in her hand.

She says, 'Thanks, but I don't smoke.'

SMOKING

Q. What do you do if your girlfriend starts smoking?
A. Slow down and use some lubricant.

SPERM COUNT

An 85-year-old man goes to his doctor to get a sperm count.

The doctor gives the man a jar and says, 'Take this jar home and bring back a semen sample tomorrow.'

The next day the old man reappears at the surgery and gives him the jar, which is still empty. The doctor asks what went wrong.

The old man says, 'First I tried with my right hand, but nothing. Then I tried with my left hand, but still nothing. Then I asked my wife for help. She tried with her right hand, then her left, still nothing. She tried with her mouth, and still nothing. We even called up the lady next door and she tried too: first with both hands, then an armpit, and she even tried squeezing it between her knees. But still nothing.'

Shocked, the doctor says, 'You asked your neighbour?'

The old man says, 'Yes. And no matter what we tried, we still couldn't get the jar open.'

SPERM HOLD-UP

A man wearing a mask bursts into a sperm bank holding a shotgun.

'Open the safe!' he yells at the woman behind the counter.

'But we're not a real bank,' she says. 'This is a sperm bank: we don't hold money.'

He says, 'Don't argue – just open the safe or I'll blow your head off.'

She obliges and opens the safe door.

He says, 'Take one of the bottles and drink it.'

She says, 'But it's full of sperm.'

He says, 'Don't argue; just drink it.'

She takes off the cap and gulps it down.

He says, 'Take out another bottle and drink it too.'

The girl drinks another one.

Suddenly the bloke pulls off the mask and, to the woman's amazement, it's her husband.

He says, 'See? Not that bloody difficult, is it?'

SPROUTS AND BUSH

Q. What do Brussels sprouts and a woman's pubic hair have in common?
A. You push them aside and carry on eating.

TONGUE

Q. What do you call a woman with her tongue sticking out?
A. A lesbian with a hard-on.

TOOTHPASTE MODEL

Q. What did the man say to the toothpaste model after she gave him a blow-job?
A. 'Those are the whitest teeth I've ever come across.'

TRAGIC THREESOME

A cruise in the Pacific goes wrong, the ship sinks and there are only three survivors: Damian, Darren and Deirdre.

They manage to swim to a small island, and they live there, doing what's natural for men and women to do.

After a couple of years, the previously chaste Deirdre feels so bad about having casual sex with two men that she kills herself.

It's a tragic time but Damian and Darren manage to get through it. They still have sexual needs, and so, after a while, nature once more takes its inevitable course.

But a couple more years later, Damian and Darren begin to feel ashamed of what they're doing.

So they bury her.

TROU FAUX

An American businessman has a meeting in France.

He meets a woman and that night they have a special kind of meeting of their own.

While they're having sex, she yells, 'Trou faux, trou faux!'

He doesn't know what that means, but assumes it to be some sort of praise.

The next day, he plays golf with the men from the meeting.

One of them hits a hole in one, so the businessman cries, 'Trou faux, trou faux!'

The other man looks at him and says, 'What do you mean, wrong hole?'

TWO EGGS

Two eggs are boiling in a saucepan.

One says to the other, 'Look, I've got a crack.'

The other says, 'No point telling me; I'm not hard yet.'

TWO SPERM

Two sperm are swimming side by side.

One turns to the other and asks, 'How much further to go?'

The other says, 'Bloody miles – we're only just past the tonsils.'

UGLY MAN

An ugly man walks into his local wearing a big grin.

The landlord says, 'What are you so happy about?'

The ugly man says, 'Well, I live by the railway. On my way home last night, I saw a young woman tied to the tracks, like in the films. I cut her free and took her back to my place. To cut a long story short, I had sex with her all night, in every room in the house.'

The landlord says, 'Fantastic! You lucky bastard. Was she pretty?'

The ugly man says, 'Dunno, I never found the head.'

VD

Q. What's worse than your doctor telling you you've got VD?
A. Your dentist telling you you've got VD.

VIAGRA CURE

A guy falls asleep on the beach for several hours and gets horrible sunburn.

He goes to the hospital and is promptly admitted after being diagnosed with second-degree burns on his legs. He's starting to blister and he's in agony.

The doctor prescribes continuous intravenous feeding with saline and electrolytes, a sedative and, every four hours, a Viagra pill.

The nurse says, 'What good will Viagra do him?'

The doctor says, 'It'll keep the sheets off his legs.'

WALRUS AND TUPPERWARE

Q. What do a walrus and Tupperware have in common?
A. They both like a tight seal.

WANT A WATCH

Little Johnny sees that his friend at school has a new watch, so he asks him how he got it.

His friend says, 'I waited until I heard the bedsprings squeaking in my parents' bedroom and then I ran in. My father gave me a watch to get rid of me.'

So Johnny goes home and waits until he hears the bedsprings squeaking and then runs into his parents' bedroom.

His father yells, 'What's up?'

Johnny says, 'I wanna watch!'

His father says, 'Well, then, sit down and shut up!'

WEARING THE TROUSERS

Dave is about to marry Davina and his father takes him to one side.

He says, 'When I married your mother, the first thing I did when we got home was take off my trousers. I gave them to your mother and told her to put them on. When she did, they were enormous on her and she said to me that she couldn't possibly wear them. I said, "Of course they're too big. I wear the trousers in this family and I always will." Ever since that day, we've never had a single problem.'

Dave takes his father's advice, and as soon as he gets Davina alone after the wedding, he does the same thing: takes off his trousers, gives them to Davina and tells her to put them on.

Davina says the trousers are too big and that she couldn't possibly wear them. Dave says, 'Exactly. I wear the trousers in this relationship and I always will. I don't want you to forget that.'

Davina pauses, removes her knickers and gives them to Dave.

She says, 'Try these on.'

He does, but they're too small.

He says, 'I can't possibly get into your knickers.'

She says, 'Exactly. And if you don't change your attitude, you never will.'

WEDDING RIOT

A young couple get married and, according to tradition in their families, the best man has the first dance with the bride.

But the couple continue to dance for the second song, too; then the third. By the time they get to the fourth, the groom rushes up and boots the bride between the legs.

There's a riot. Eventually all the guests are hauled off by the police to appear in court.

The judge asks the best man what happened.

'Your honour,' says the best man, 'we were just dancing, and the groom ran up and booted the bride between the legs.'

'That must have hurt,' says the judge.

'It certainly did,' said the best man, 'it broke three of my fingers!'

WHALES

Two whales overturn a ship using their blowholes.

'Can we eat the crew?' asks one.

'No,' says the other. 'I do blow-jobs but I don't swallow seamen.'

WIFE'S PRESENTS

For Christmas, my wife asked for something long, thin and hard with a rubber on the end.

So I brought her the finest pencil money could buy.

For her birthday, she asked for something around six inches with a head on it.

So I gave her a tenner.

WIVES

An Italian, a Frenchman and an Englishman are in the pub, chatting about their wives.

The Italian says, 'I made love to my wife last night, and straight after I kissed her feet – she rose six inches off the bed.'

The Frenchman says, 'That's nothing. I made love to my wife last night, and straight after I licked the inside of her thighs – she rose 12 inches off the bed.'

The English bloke says, 'Oh, yeah? Well, I knobbed my missus last night, shot my bolt, wiped my cock on the curtains and she hit the roof!'

WOMEN AND FRIDGES

Q. What's the difference between a woman and a fridge?
A. A fridge doesn't fart when you pull your meat out.

WOMEN AND POLICE CARS

Q. What do women and police cars have in common?
A. They both make a lot of noise to let you know they're coming.

BLOKES

ADAM

Adam came first.
But then, men always do.

ALWAYS THERE

A woman's husband has been slipping in and out of a coma for months, yet she's stayed by his bedside every single day.

One day, he awakes and whispers, 'It's amazing. Though all my bad times, you've been with me. When I got fired, you were there. When I got shot, you were by my side. When I lost a leg in a car crash, you were there. When we lost the house, you stayed. When my health started failing, you were still by my side. You know what?'

She says, 'What, darling?'

He says, 'You must be bad luck: piss off.'

BANKERS

Q. Why are bankers good in bed?
A. They know the penalty for early withdrawal.

Black Eyes

A bloke with a black eye boards a plane.

He notices the bloke next to him has a black eye, too. He says, 'Mind if I ask how you got yours?'

The other bloke says, 'It was a tongue-twister accident. I was at the ticket counter and I got served by a blonde with huge breasts. Instead of saying, "I'd like two tickets to Pittsburgh", I accidentally said, "I'd like two pickets to Tittsburgh". So she belted me.'

The first bloke says, 'Wow! mine was a tongue-twister too. I was at breakfast this morning and I wanted to say to my wife, "Please pour me a bowl of Frosties, darling". But I accidentally said, "You ruined my life, you evil slag".'

BIG MOLE

A bloke goes to the pub to meet his mate.

He says, 'Sorry I haven't been in touch for a few days – I've been in the hospital getting a dirty great mole removed from the end of my cock.'

His mate says, 'Sounds painful.'

He says, 'Too right – that's the last time I shag one of those little buggers.'

BLIND NUDIST

Q. How do you find a blind man in a nudist colony?
A. It's not hard.

BLINKING

Q. Why don't women blink during foreplay?
A. They don't have time.

BRAINS

Q. Why were men given larger brains than dogs?
A. So they wouldn't hump women's legs at parties.

BUBBLE BATH

Q. How does a man take a bubble bath?
A. He eats baked beans for dinner.

CAR INSURANCE

Q. Why do men pay more than women for car insurance?
A. Because women don't get blow-jobs while they're driving.

CHEAP HOTEL AND TIGHT PANTS

Q. What do a cheap hotel and a tight pair of pants have in common?
A. No ballroom.

CIRCUMCISER

Did you hear about the short-sighted circumciser?
   He got the sack.

CLINGFILM

A bloke walks into a psychiatrist's office wearing only clingfilm.
   The shrink says, 'I can clearly see you're nuts.'

CLITORIS AND MORE

Q. What do a clitoris, a woman's birthday and a toilet have in common?
A. Men always miss them.

NEW MOBILE PHONE TECHNOLOGY WILL
ALLOW MANKIND TO SHARE IDEAS, PASSIONS
AND THOUGHTS IN A WAY UNIMAGINED
BY THEIR ANCESTORS

COCK CLOCKS

A cowboy is riding on the plains.

He comes across a Red Indian boy lying naked on his back with a huge erection.

The cowboy says, 'What the hell are you doing?'

The Indian looks at the shadow of his cock and says, 'It's 1pm.'

The cowboy rides on.

Soon he runs into another Red Indian. He too is lying on his back naked with a huge erection.

The cowboy says, 'What the hell are you doing?'

The Indian looks at the shadow of his cock and says, 'It's 2.30pm.'

The cowboy rides on.

Later he comes upon a third Red Indian. This one is lying on his back naked, masturbating.

The cowboy says, 'Christ! What the hell are you doing?'

The Indian says, 'I'm winding my watch.'

COLOURS

Q. Why is a man's urine yellow and his sperm white?
A. So he can tell if he's coming or going.

COMA CURE

Some nurses are bathing a woman in a coma when one of them notices a slight response on the monitor when they touch her genitals.

So they go to her husband and say, 'Crazy as this sounds, maybe a little oral sex will bring her out of the coma.'

The husband is sceptical, but they assure him that with the curtains closed for privacy it might just work. He finally agrees and goes into his wife's room.

A few minutes pass and then the woman's monitor flat-lines and the alarm starts ringing. The nurses burst into the room.

'What happened?' they cry.

The husband says, 'I think she choked.'

COWBOY'S WISHES

A cowboy is taken prisoner by a group of Red Indians.

The Indians are ready to kill him when the chief announces

that because of the Celebration of the Great Spirit, they'll grant the cowboy three wishes before he dies.

The chief says, 'What do you want for your first wish?'

The cowboy says, 'I want to talk to my horse.'

So he goes over to his horse and whispers in its ear.

The horse neighs and takes off at speed.

About an hour later, it returns with a naked lady on its back.

The chief says, 'What do you want for your second wish?'

The cowboy says, 'I want to talk to my horse again.'

So again he whispers in the horse's ear. The horse neighs and takes off at speed.

About an hour later, the horse comes back with another naked lady on its back.

Then the chief says, 'What do you want for your last wish?'

The cowboy says, 'I want to talk to my horse again.'

He grabs the horse by the ears and yells, 'You stupid animal: I said "Posse!"'

CROSS THE ROAD

Q. Why did the man cross the road?
A. He heard the chicken was a slut.

DIE BEFORE YOUR WIFE

Q. Why do men die before their wives?
A. They want to.

DIFFERENCE

Q. What's the difference between men and women?
A. A woman wants one man to satisfy her every need. A man wants every woman to satisfy his one need.

DISAPPOINTMENT

Q. Why is the book Women Who Love Too Much a disappointment for male readers?
A. No phone numbers.

DREAMS

Three men on a road trip have to stay the night at a hotel and, short of money, end up sharing a bed.

In the morning the guy who'd slept on the left says, 'Wow, I had a great dream last night. I was being given a hand-job by the most beautiful woman.'

The man who'd slept on the right says, 'That's strange; I had the exact same dream.'

The man who'd slept in the middle says, 'Well, I dreamed I was skiing.'

DRUNK DRIVER

After a night out, a bloke and his date are driving home in his car when they get pulled over by the police. The policeman says to the bloke, 'Have you been drinking, sir?'

Surprised, the bloke says, 'To be honest, yes. But I was driving carefully. How could you tell?'

'Your driving was fine,' says the policeman. 'It was the fat, ugly bird in the passenger seat that gave you away.'

EGGS

Q. What's the difference between an egg and a wank?
A. You can't beat a wank.

ELEPHANT AND NAKED MAN

Q. What did the elephant say to the naked man?
A. 'How do you breathe through something so small?'

ELEPHANT ASSAULT

A man goes to his doctor and says, 'Doctor, I've just been raped by an elephant. My arsehole has been stretched this wide.'

The doctor says, 'Bend over and let me have a look.'

The bloke bends over and sure enough, his arsehole is about 10 inches across.

'But I thought an elephant's cock was long and thin?' says the doctor.

'Yes, it was,' says the man, 'but the bastard fingered me first.'

EYE CONTACT

Q. Why do men find it difficult to make eye contact?
A. Breasts don't have eyes.

FOREPLAY

Q. What's a man's idea of foreplay?
A. Half an hour of begging.

FORESKIN SURGERY

A boy born with no eyelids is to have pioneering surgery using foreskins.

His parents are hoping it won't leave him cock-eyed.

GETTING OLD

Q. How do you know when you're getting old?
A. When you start having dry dreams and wet farts.

GIRLFRIEND'S TASTE

Q. How does a Welshman improve his girlfriend's taste?
A. By adding mint sauce.

GOD

Q. Why did God create men?
A. Because a vibrator can't mow the lawn.

Elephant's Erection

Mummy takes little Johnny to the zoo. At the elephant enclosure, the elephant has an erection.

'What's that?' asks little Johnny.

'It's nothing,' says the embarrassed mother.

A week later, Johnny's dad takes him and the same thing happens.

'What's that?' asks Johnny.

'A 24-inch penis,' replies dad.

'Mummy said it was nothing,' says Johnny.

His dad says, 'Well, son, your mother's spoilt.'

GOD AND ADAM

God calls Adam and says, 'I have some good news and some bad news. Which would you like to hear first?'

Adam says, 'The good news.'

God says, 'I've given you a penis and a brain.'

Adam says, 'What's the bad news?'

God says, 'I only gave you enough blood to operate one at a time.'

GREATEST ATHLETE

Q. Who's the world's greatest athlete?

A. The bloke who finishes both first and third in a masturbation contest.

GENETIC INFORMATION MAPPING

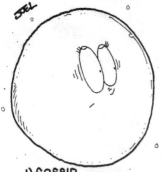

1) GOSSIP

2) EMOTIONAL MATURITY

3) DOING MORE THAN ONE THING AT ONCE

1) FOOTBALL STATISTICS

2) FIGHTING

3) GADGETS

4) FORGETTING TO PUT THE BINS OUT

HARD AND LIGHT

Q. What's the difference between hard and light?
A. You can go to sleep with a light on.

INSENSITIVE BIT

Q. What do you call the insensitive bit at the base of the penis?
A. The man.

IRISH DROWNING

A policeman comes to tell an Irish woman about her husband's untimely drowning in a vat of beer at the brewery.

She sobs, 'Oh, the poor man. Please, tell me: did he suffer much?'

The policeman says, 'I don't think so; he came out three times to piss.'

HOLE

Q. Why is there a hole in a bloke's penis?
A. So he can get air to his brain.

ICY CONDOM

Q. Why did the Irishman put ice in his condom?
A. To bring the swelling down.

IN THE BEGINNING

In the beginning, God created Earth and rested. Then God created man and rested. Then God created woman.

Since then, neither God nor man has rested.

LAUNDRY

Q. How do men sort their laundry?
A. 'Dirty' and 'Dirty but wearable'.

LOTTERY WINNER

A bloke comes running through the front door of his house screaming, 'I've won the lottery! Pack your bags!'

His wife says, 'Great! What shall I pack?'

He says, 'I don't care; just get the fuck out of my house!'

MAKE HIM SICK

A police officer finds a bloke in an alley with his finger up another man's arse.

'What are you doing?' asks the policeman.

'It's all right,' says the bloke. 'He's been drinking and I'm trying to make him sick.'

'You won't make him sick by shoving your finger up his arse,' says the policeman.

The bloke says, 'I will when I put it in his mouth.'

NAKED MEN

Q. What do you call 12 naked men sitting on each other's shoulders?
A. A scrotum pole.

"I can't get it in."

NAKED WOMAN

A bloke moves into a new flat, and goes to the lobby to put his name on the group letterbox.

While he's there, an attractive young woman comes out of the flat next to the letterboxes, wearing only a dressing-gown.

The bloke smiles at the woman and she strikes up a conversation with him. As they talk, her dressing-gown slips open, and it's obvious she's got nothing on underneath.

The poor bloke breaks into a sweat trying to maintain eye contact.

After a few minutes, the woman places her hand on his arm and says, 'Let's go in my flat; I hear someone coming...'

He follows her into the flat, and after she closes the door, she leans against it, allowing her dressing-gown to fall off completely.

Completely naked, she purrs, 'What would you say is the best part of my body?'

Blushing, the bloke says, 'It's got to be your ears.'

Astounded, the woman says, 'My ears? Look at my breasts! They're big, don't sag, and they're completely natural. My bum is firm and has no cellulite on it. Look at my skin – no spots or scars. Why the hell would you say my ears are the best part of my body?'

The bloke says, 'You know outside when you said you heard someone coming? That was me.'

NUN'S PUNISHMENT

Three men are travelling and looking for a place to stay. Eventually they come across a convent and ask the Mother Superior if they can stay the night.

She says, 'If I catch you looking at my nuns in the showers, I'll have to cut your dicks off.'

Sure enough, they get caught, and she asks the first man, 'What's your job?'

'A butcher.'

'Then I'll cut your dick off with a knife.'

The second guy says he's a joiner, so the nun says, 'I'll cut yours off with a saw.'

Finally she turns to the third man and says the same, to which he replies, 'I'm a lollipop man. What are you gonna do – suck it?'

NURSING HOME

A man puts his father in a nursing home.

The old man cries, 'Please don't put me in there, son.'

The son says, 'Dad, I can't take care of you. I've checked the place out and it's the best there is. I think you'll love it.'

The next day the old man calls his son and says, 'Son, you were right! I love this place.'

The son says, 'Glad to hear it. What makes it so great?'

The old man says, 'Last night I was in my room and from out of nowhere, I got an erection. A nurse came in, saw my hard-on and gave me a blow-job! I haven't had one of those in 30 years! I'd almost forgotten what it was like! It was fantastic!'

A few days later, the old man calls his son again and says, 'You have to get me out of here. I hate this place.'

The son says, 'What's wrong?'

The old man says, 'Last night I fell down in the corridor. While I was still on my hands and knees, a male nurse came along and took me up the arse. I can't go on like this.'

The son says, 'Dad, I know that's terrible and we'll get it sorted out, but until then, you have to take the rough with the smooth.'

The old man says, 'No, you don't understand. I get an erection maybe once a year, but I fall down two or three times a day.'

PEEPING TOM AND A THIEF

Q. What's the difference between a peeping tom and a thief?
A. A thief snatches watches.

PENIS OP

John goes to the doctors and says, 'Doctor, you've got to help me – I just can't get a hard-on.'

So the doctor examines his cock and says, 'Your cock muscles are too weak. We're going to have to take the muscles from an elephant's cock and graft them on to your penis.'

John's desperate for sex, so he agrees.

After the op, John goes out on a dinner date with a new girl. But half-way through the meal, his cock starts to feel strange and uncomfortably big, so to release the strain he unzips his flies under the table.

Suddenly his cock springs out of his trousers, grabs a bun from the next table and shoots back into his trousers with it.

His date is stunned and says, 'Christ, you've got a huge cock. Can you do that again?'

John replies, 'Well, I could try, but I don't think I can fit another bun up my arse.'

PENIS PROBLEM

Jeff walks into a pub and sees his friend Paul slumped miserably at the bar. He goes over to ask what's wrong.

'Well,' says Paul. 'You know that beautiful girl at work who I wanted to ask out, but couldn't because I got an embarrassing erection every time I saw her?'

'Yes,' says Jeff.

'I finally plucked up the courage to ask her out, and she agreed.'

'That's great,' says Jeff. 'When are you going out?'

'I went to meet her this evening,' says Paul, 'but I was worried I'd get an erection again. So I got some duct tape and taped my penis to my leg, so that if I did get a hard-on, it wouldn't show.'

'Good thinking,' says Jeff.

'So I get to her door,' says Paul, 'and I rang the doorbell. She answered it in the tiniest dress you ever saw.'

'And what happened then?'

'I kicked her in the face.'

PLASTIC SURGERY

Two old friends meet for the first time in 40 years.

The first says, 'Bill, you look like you did 40 years ago. What's your secret?'

Bill replies, 'Plastic surgery. It's really great, but now my belly-button is at the back of my head.'

His friend looks disgusted.

Bill says, 'If you think that's weird, you should see what I'm wearing as a tie.'

POISONED PENIS

Two blokes are walking through the jungle when the first is bitten on the penis by a snake.

Quickly, the second bloke rings the emergency services on his mobile.

'My friend's been bitten by a snake,' he cries. 'What can I do?'

The operator says, 'Is it a poisonous snake?'

'Yes, a tiger snake,' says the second bloke.

'Then you must immediately suck the poison out, or your friend will be dead within an hour.'

The second bloke hangs up and says, 'Sorry, mate – he says you'll be dead within an hour.'

Quiet Night

Two married blokes are out drinking one night when one says, 'I don't know what else to do. Whenever I go home after we've been out drinking, I turn the headlights off before I get to the driveway. I shut off the engine and coast into the garage. I take my shoes off before I go into the house. I sneak up the stairs. I get undressed in the bathroom. I ease into bed... and my wife still wakes up and yells, "And what time do you call this"?'

His mate looks at him and says, 'Well, you're obviously taking the wrong approach. I screech into the driveway, slam the door, clatter up the steps, chuck my shoes against the wall, jump into bed, slap my wife's arse and say, "How about a blow-job"? And she's always sound asleep.'

PUBLIC TOILETS

Q. Why are blokes like public toilets?
A. They're either vacant, engaged or full of crap.

SAFE SEX 1

Q. How do men practise safe sex?
A. They meet their bit on the side at least 10 miles from where they live.

SAFE SEX 2

Q. What is a man's definition of safe sex?
A. A padded headboard.

SCOTSMAN'S KILT

Q. What does a Scotsman wear under his kilt?
A. Lipstick, on a good day.

SECOND DATE

Q. What do you call a man who expects to have sex on the second date?
A. Slow.

SELF-PLEASURE

Q. Why do men masturbate?
A. It's sex with someone they love.

SEX AND DRIVING

Q. Why are men so bad at sex and driving?
A. Because they always pull out with no thought of who else might be coming.

SEX DISEASE

Big Gay Glenn goes to the doctor and has some tests.

The doctor comes back and says, 'Glenn, I'm not going to beat about the bush. You have AIDS.'

Glenn is devastated. 'Doctor, what can I do?'

'Eat one sausage, one head of cabbage, 20 unpeeled carrots drenched in hot sauce, 10 Jalapeno peppers, 40 walnuts, 40 peanuts, half a box of Grape Nuts, and top it off with a gallon of prune juice.'

Glenn asks, 'Will that cure me, Doctor?'

The doctor says, 'No, but it should leave you with a better understanding of what your arse is for.'

SEX DRUG

A bloke walks into a chemist and says to the assistant, 'I have three girls coming over tonight. I've never had three at once, so I need something to keep me horny.'

The chemist gives him a box of mysterious pills marked with an 'X' and says, 'Here, if you eat these you'll be rock-hard for 12 hours.'

The bloke says, 'Brilliant! Give me three boxes.'

The next day, the bloke walks into the same chemist and pulls down his trousers. The assistant looks in horror as he notices the man's cock is black and blue, with skin hanging off in places.

The man says, 'Give me a bottle of Deep Heat.'

The assistant says, 'Deep Heat? You're not going to put Deep Heat on that, are you?'

The man says, 'No, it's for my arms – the girls didn't show up.'

SEXUALLY AROUSED

Q. How can you tell if a man's sexually aroused?
A. He's breathing.

SHAKES

Three old men are complaining about how much their hands shake.

The first old bloke says, 'My hands shake so bad that when I shaved this morning, I cut my face.'

The second old bloke says, 'Oh, yeah? Well, my hands shake so bad that when I trimmed my garden yesterday, I sliced all my flowers.'

The third old bloke says, 'That's nothing. My hands shake so bad that when I took a piss yesterday, I came three times.'

AFTER PULLING STACEY IN THE NIGHTCLUB, DAVE WISHED HE HADN'T LEFT IT TILL THE NEXT MORNING TO FIND OUT WHAT "POST-OP TRANSEXUAL" MEANT

SHEEP IN LONG GRASS

Q. How does a Welshman find a sheep in long grass?
A. Irresistible.

SHOP FLASHER

A bloke goes into a jeweller's, unzips his flies and pulls out his penis.

Unfazed, the saleswoman says, 'This is a clock shop, not a cock shop.'

The bloke says, 'OK, put two hands on it.'

SHOWERS AND BATHS

Q. Why do men take showers instead of baths?
A. Pissing in the bath is disgusting.

SICK BROTHEL

A bloke goes into a brothel with a tenner.

'Sorry, mate,' says the pimp, 'the only thing you can have for a tenner is a goat.'

The bloke shrugs, pays his money and shags the goat.

The next week he returns to the brothel – but this time he's only got a fiver.

'Sorry,' says the pimp, 'but all you can get for a fiver is a peep show.'

So he goes into the peep show and there's a load of blokes spying on a guy wanking off a gorilla.

'Jesus,' says the first bloke. 'I've never seen anything like this before.'

'You should have been here last week,' says the bloke next to him. 'There was a guy in there shagging a goat.'

SPEAKING TO YOUR WIFE

One bloke says to another, 'I haven't spoken to my wife for 18 months.'

The other bloke says, 'Why not?'

The first bloke says, 'I don't like to interrupt her.'

SPINE

Q. Why do men have a spine?

A. If they didn't, they'd suck their cocks all day long.

TAX INSPECTOR

At the end of the tax year, the Tax Office sends an inspector to audit the books of a synagogue.

While he's checking the books, he says to the Rabbi, 'I notice you buy a lot of candles. What do you do with the candle drippings?'

The Rabbi says, 'We save them up and send them back to the candle-makers, and every now and then they send us a complete box of candles.'

The tax inspector says, 'What about all these matzo balls you buy? What do you do with the crumbs?'

The Rabbi says, 'We collect them and send them back to the manufacturers, and every now and then they send a complete box of matzo balls.'

The tax inspector says, 'And what do you do with all the leftover foreskins from the circumcisions you perform?'

The Rabbi says, 'Here, too, we do not waste. We save up all the foreskins and send them to the Tax Office, and about once a year they send us a complete dick.'

TRAINS AND BREASTS

Q. What do toy train sets and breasts have in common?
A. They're usually intended for children, but it's the men who end up playing with them.

TRANSSEXUAL

A little boy asks his father, 'Dad, what is a transsexual?'
His father says, 'Ask your mother; he'll know.'

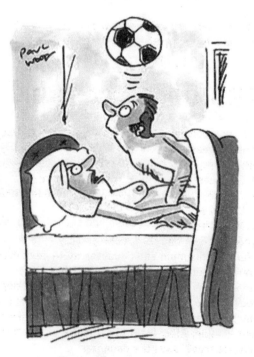

"Don't you ever think of anything else Brian!?"

TWO GEEKS

Two IT guys are walking through the park when one says, 'Where did you get such a great bike?'

The second IT guy says, 'I was walking along yesterday, minding my own business, when a beautiful woman rode up on this bike. She threw the bike to the ground, took off all her clothes and said, "Take what you want".

The second IT guy nods approvingly and says, 'Good choice – the clothes probably wouldn't have fitted.'

TWO TESTICLES

Q. What did the left testicle say to the right testicle?
A. Dunno, but they were talking bollocks.

TYPES OF BREASTS

One day, at the dinner table, a son asks his father, 'Dad, how many kinds of breasts are there?'

The father says, 'Son, there are three types. In her twenties, a woman's breasts are like melons, round and firm. In her thirties to forties, they're like pears, still nice but drooping a bit. After 50, they're like onions.'

'Onions?' says the son.

'Yes, you see them and they make you cry.'

This infuriates his mum and daughter, so the daughter says, 'Mum, how many kinds of penises are there?'

The mother looks at her husband and says, 'Well, dear, a man goes through three phases. In his twenties, his penis is like an oak, mighty and hard. In his thirties to forties, it's like a birch, flexible but reliable. After his fifties, it's like a Christmas tree.'

'A Christmas tree?' says the daughter.

'Yes, dead from the root up and the balls are for decoration only.'

UGLY WOMEN

One bloke asks another, 'Have you ever gone to bed with an ugly woman?'

The second bloke says, 'No, but I've woken up with plenty.'

ULTIMATE REJECTION

Q. What's the ultimate rejection?
A. Your hand falling asleep as you masturbate.

WANDERING HANDS

A gorgeous woman wanders over to the bar in a pub. She seductively signals at the barman to bring his face close to hers, then reaches out her hands and caresses his beard.

'Are you the manager?' she purrs, stroking his face.

'No,' he replies, wide-eyed.

'Can you get him for me?' she whispers, running her hands through his hair.

'I'm afraid I can't,' he breathes, clearly aroused. 'Is there anything I can do?'

'Yes,' she continues huskily, popping a couple of fingers into his mouth for him to suck. 'Tell him there's no loo paper or soap in the ladies' toilets.'

WOMEN AND COMPUTERS

Q. What's the difference between a woman and a computer?
A. A woman won't accept a three-and-a-half-inch floppy.

YOUR MUM

Two blokes are in a pub.
   One says to the other, 'I shagged your mum.'
   The other doesn't reply.
   Again the first one shouts, 'I shagged your mum.'
   The whole pub turns round to watch.
   The other bloke says, 'Go home, Dad, you're drunk.'

YOUR ROUND

Two blokes are in the pub. One says to the other, 'Your round.'
   The other replies, 'So are you, you fat bastard.'

WOMEN

ANAL DEODORANT

A blonde walks into a chemist's and asks the assistant for some anal deodorant.

The chemist, a little bemused, explains to the woman that they don't sell anal deodorant, and never have done.

Unfazed, the blonde assures the chemist she's often bought the stuff from this shop and would like some more.

'I'm sorry,' says the chemist. 'Do you have the container it came in?'

'Yes,' says the blonde, producing it from her handbag.

The chemist says, 'But this is just a normal stick of under-arm deodorant.'

The blonde replies, 'But the label says, "To apply, push up bottom".'

ANNOY YOUR GIRLFRIEND

Q. How do you annoy your girlfriend during sex?
A. Phone her.

BANANA AND VIBRATOR

A banana and a vibrator are sitting on a woman's bedside table.

The banana says, 'I don't know why you're shaking; she's going to bloody eat me.'

BEER HORMONES

Scientists have discovered beer contains female hormones.

In tests, they gave three men 12 pints each, and they all talked crap, gained weight and couldn't drive.

BIG PROBLEM

A blonde visits her gynaecologist.

He peers between her legs. 'Christ, you've got a big vagina... Christ, you've got a big vagina.'

She says, 'You don't need to say it twice.'

He says, 'I didn't.'

BLONDE AND THE PILL

Q. Why did the blonde stop using the Pill?

A. Because it kept falling out.

BLONDE GOES SHOPPING

A blonde walks into a shop and asks the bloke behind the counter if she can buy a picture frame.

The bloke says, 'Do you wanna screw for it?'

The blonde says, 'No, but I'll give you a blow-job for that lampshade.'

BLONDES AND COMPUTERS

Q. How can you tell if a blonde's used your computer?
A. The joystick's wet.

BLONDES AND CUPBOARDS

Q. What's the difference between a blonde and a stationery cupboard?
A. You can only fit two men at once in a stationery cupboard.

BLONDES AND IRONING BOARDS

Q. What's the difference between a blonde and an ironing board?
A. An ironing board's legs are difficult to part.

BLONDES AND THE TITANIC

Q. What's the difference between a blonde and the Titanic?
A. Only 1,500 went down on the Titanic.

BLONDES AND TRACKS

Q. Why is a blonde like a railway track?
A. Because she's been laid all over the country.

BLONDES AND WASHING MACHINES

Q. Why is a blonde like an old washing machine?
A. They both drip when they're fucked.

BLONDE'S BREAKDOWN

A blonde pushes her BMW into a petrol station.

She tells the mechanic the engine's died. After he's worked on it for a few minutes, it's running smoothly again.

She says, 'What's the story?'

He replies, 'Just crap in the carburettor.'

She says, 'OK, how often do I have to do that?'

BLONDE'S CAR CRASH

A blonde is involved in a serious car crash.

The paramedics arrive and drag her out of the car, lying her flat on the ground.

The first paramedic says, 'I'm going to check if you're concussed. How many fingers am I putting up?'

The blonde says, 'Oh, my God – I'm paralysed from the waist down!'

BLONDE'S DRESS

A blonde walks into the dry cleaners.

She places a garment on the counter and says, 'I'll be back tomorrow afternoon to pick up my dress.'

'Come again?' says the deaf old assistant, cupping his ear.

'No,' she says, 'this time it's mayonnaise.'

Blonde's Kids

A blonde goes to the council to register for child benefit.

'How many children?' asks the council worker.

'Ten,' says the blonde.

'Ten?' says the council worker. 'What are their names?'

'Wayne, Wayne, Wayne, Wayne, Wayne, Wayne, Wayne, Wayne, Wayne and Wayne.'

'Doesn't that get confusing?'

'No,' says the blonde. 'It's great, because if they're out playing in the street I just have to shout, "Wayne, your dinner's ready" or, "Wayne, go to bed now", and they all do it.'

'But what if you want to speak to one individually?' asks the council worker.

'Easy,' says the blonde. 'I just use their surnames.'

BLONDES' EARS

Q. What do blondes put behind their ears to attract blokes?
A. Their knees.

BLONDE'S FIRST TIME

A bloke picks up a young blonde and takes her back to his hotel room.
   After they have sex, he says, 'Am I the first man you've had sex with?'
   She says, 'You might be; your face looks familiar.'

BLONDE'S FLOWERS

Two blondes meet up.
   The first one says, 'My boyfriend bought me a bunch of flowers on Friday evening. I had to keep my legs open all weekend.'
   The other says, 'Why? Didn't you have a vase?'

BLONDES' KNICKERS

Q. Why do blondes wear knickers?
A. To keep their ankles warm.

BLONDE'S LETTERS

A blonde and an Irishman are in a pub when the blonde notices something strange about the wellies the Irishman is wearing.

She says, 'Why does one of your wellies have an L written on it, while the other has an R?'

The Irishman says, 'It helps me remember. The one with the L is my left boot and the one with the R is my right.'

'Ah,' says the blonde, 'so that's why my knickers have got C&A on them.'

BLONDE'S LIGHT

Q. How does a blonde turn on the light after sex?
A. She opens the car door.

"Now all she needs is a brain.
Of course if we can't find one,
we could always dye her hair
blonde I suppose."

BLONDES' NURSERY RHYME

Q. What nursery rhyme do blondes learn as kids?
A. Hump Me Dump Me.

BLONDE'S ODD BREASTS

Q. Why did the blonde have rectangular breasts?
A. She forgot to take the tissues out of the box.

BLONDE'S ORGASMS

Q. What does a blonde say after multiple orgasms?
A. 'Thanks, team!'

BLONDE'S THERAPIST

A blonde says to her therapist, 'Kiss me, kiss me!'
   The therapist says, 'No, that's unethical. I shouldn't even be shagging you.'

BLONDE'S VIBRATOR

A blonde enters a sex shop and asks for a vibrator.
   The assistant says, 'Choose from our range on the wall.'
   She says, 'I'll take the big red one.'
   The assistant says, 'That's a fire extinguisher.'

BLOW-JOB BONUS

Q. What's the best thing about a blow-job?
A. Five minutes' silence.

BOTTLE-BLONDES AND PLANES

Q. What do bottle-blondes and airliners have in common?
A. They both have black boxes.

BREAST EXERCISES

A bloke arrives home to find his wife in front of a mirror stretching her arms, chanting, 'I must, I must improve my bust.'
The bloke says, 'What are you doing?'
His wife says, 'An exercise to make my boobs bigger.'
The bloke says, 'That doesn't work. What you need to do is rub toilet paper between them.'
His wife says, 'And that will make them bigger?'
The bloke says, 'Well, it worked on your arse.'

BREASTS LIKE MELONS

Two gynaecologists meet up.
One says, 'I had a patient today with breasts like melons.'
The other says, 'Wow, that big?'
'Yes, that big.'
'Well, I had a patient with a clitoris like a lemon.'
'Wow, that big?'
'No, that sour.'

BURNT BLONDE

Q. How do you make a blonde burn her face?
A. Ring her when she's doing the ironing.

CHEATING GIRLFRIEND

A bloke comes home to find his girlfriend having sex with his best mate.

He says, 'What's going on here?'

The girlfriend turns to the mate and says, 'See? I told you he was stupid.'

"Do you ever regret having breast implants when you were younger?"

CIRCUMCISION

Q. Why do women like circumcised cocks?
A. They can't resist anything with 10 per cent off.

COMPETITION WINNER

Did you hear about the woman with no arms and no legs who won the strawberry-picking competition?
   Jammy twat.

DAUGHTER'S BOYFRIEND

A man doesn't like his daughter's boyfriend and decides to confront her.
   'That boyfriend of yours isn't good enough for you,' he says. 'He's the stupidest bloke I've ever met.'
   'Daddy,' she replies, 'he's not stupid. We've only been together nine weeks and already he's cured that little illness I used to have every month.'

DESIGNING WOMEN

Q. Who helped God design woman?
A. The council – who else would put a playground next to a shithole?

FARTS

Q. Why do men fart more often than women?
A. Because women can't shut up long enough to build up the required pressure.

FAT WOMAN

A fat woman says to her gynaecologist, 'I don't enjoy sex any more.'

The gynaecologist says, 'Why don't you diet?'

The woman says, 'OK, then – can you recommend a colour?'

FEMALE ARCHAEOLOGIST

Q. How do you piss off a female archaeologist?
A. Show her a used tampon and ask her which period it came from.

FIVE POUNDS OF FAT

Q. What makes five pounds of fat look really good?
A. A nipple.

FOXES AND ROTTWEILERS

Q. How do you turn a fox into a Rottweiler?
A. Marry her.

GIRLFRIEND AND WIFE

Q. What's the difference between a girlfriend and a wife?
A. About two stone.

"Do you do brain enlargements?"

GIRLFRIEND'S BIRTHDAY

It's my girlfriend's birthday soon, so I bought her a handbag and a dildo.

If she doesn't like the handbag, she can go fuck herself.

GIRL SEES TACKLE

Little Annie wanders into the bathroom while her dad is in the bath.

She looks down at his tackle and says, 'What's that, Daddy?'

Her dad looks sheepish and replies, 'Er... it's my hedgehog, darling.'

Little Annie says, 'Christ, it's got a big dick.'

Graveyard Wreath

Two women walking home drunk need to pee, so they duck into a graveyard.

They don't have any toilet paper, so the first woman uses her knickers, then throws them away. The other finds a ribbon from a wreath and uses that.

The next day their husbands are talking. The first says, 'We'd better keep an eye on our wives. Mine came home last night with no knickers on.'

The second says, 'You think that's bad? Mine had a card stuck on her arse that said, "From all the lads at the fire station; we'll never forget you".'

GIRL'S HAIRCUT

A little girl goes to the barber with her father.

She stands next to the barber's chair, eating a cake while her dad gets his hair cut.

The barber smiles at her and says, 'Sweetheart, you're going to get hair on your muffin.'

'I know,' she says. 'I'm gonna get tits, too.'

HANDY WOMAN

What woman can wash up with her left hand, dry up with her right, mop with one leg and dust with the other, while giving a blow-job and opening you a beer with her arse?

A Swiss army wife.

HIGH SPERM COUNT

Q. How can you tell you have a high sperm count?
A. Your girlfriend has to chew before she swallows.

LESBIAN'S CHECK-UP

'Everything looks neat and tidy in there,' says the gynaecologist to the lesbian.

'So it should be,' says the lesbian. 'I have a woman in twice a week.'

LESBIAN DINOSAUR

Q. What do you call a lesbian dinosaur?
A. A lickalotapuss.

LESBIAN TRAINERS

Nike have developed a new pair of trainers for lesbians called Nikes For Dykes.

They come with an extra-long tongue and you can get them off with one finger.

MACHO WOMAN

Q. How do you spot a macho woman?
A. She's rolling her own tampons.

"It's a period property."

MAKING LOVE

Q. How do you define "making love"?
A. Something a woman does while a bloke is shagging her.

NAKED NUNS

Two nuns are decorating the vestry and to save getting paint on their habits, they decide to do it in the nude.

Suddenly there's a knock at the door.

'Who is it?' asks Sister Mary, looking shocked.

'It's the blind man,' comes the reply from behind the door.

'Oh, that's OK,' says Sister Angelica, 'let him in.'

Sister Mary opens the door and as the bloke enters he says, 'Nice tits, love – now, where do you want these blinds?'

NIPPLE BUMPS

Q. What are the small bumps around a woman's nipples?
A. It's Braille for 'Suck here'.

NUNS IN A SHOP

Q. What do you call 100 nuns in a shop?
A. A Virgin Megastore.

OLD WOMAN ON THE BUS

Two old women are having coffee when one asks the other, 'Did you come on the bus?'

The other one says, 'Yes, but I managed to make it look like an asthma attack.'

PARALYSED WOMAN

What's it called when a woman is paralysed from the waist down?
  Marriage.

PERIOD PAINS

Q. Why do women call period pains PMS?
A. Mad Cow Disease was already taken.

PERSIAN RUGS

A lady walks into a shop which sells Persian rugs.
  She spots the perfect rug and walks over to inspect it. As she bends over to feel its texture, she farts loudly.
  Embarrassed, she looks around to see if anyone has noticed. Standing nearby is a salesman.
  He says, 'Good day, madam. How may we help you?'
  Uncomfortably, she says, 'What's the price of this rug?'
  He says, 'Madam, if you farted just touching it, you'll shit yourself when you hear the price.'

PREGNANT SHEILA

Bruce is driving over the Sydney Harbour Bridge one day when he sees his girlfriend about to throw herself off.
  Bruce slams on the brakes and yells, 'Sheila, what the hell are you doing?'
  Sheila turns round with a tear in her eye and says, 'G'day, Bruce. You got me pregnant and so now I'm gonna kill myself.'
  Bruce gets a lump in his throat when he hears this and says, 'Strewth, Sheila – not only are you a great shag, you're a real sport, too.'

PROSTITUTES AND DEALERS

Q. What's the difference between a drug dealer and a prostitute?
A. A prostitute can wash her crack and sell it again.

REASON FOR PENISES

Q. Why did God give men penises?
A. So they'd have a way to stop a woman talking.

RUBBING EYES

Q. Why do women rub their eyes when they wake up?
A. Because they don't have bollocks to scratch.

Sex toy story

SCREWING OLD LADIES

Q. What's got 100 balls and screws old ladies?
A. Bingo.

SMILING BRIDE

Q. Why does the bride always smile on her wedding day?
A. Because she knows she's given her last blow-job.

"You'd never believe it. I got replaced by a woman at work today."

STRONG GUST

A blonde is waiting for a bus when a strong gust of wind lifts her skirt and reveals she isn't wearing any knickers.

A nearby bloke, wanting to put her at ease, jokes, 'Airy, isn't it?'

'Well, what did you expect?' she replies. 'Feathers?'

SUCKING A GOLF BALL

Q. What do you call a woman who can suck a golf ball through a hose?

A. 'Darling.'

TATTOOED PROSTITUTE

Q. What do you call a tattooed prostitute?

A. A scenic root.

TORNADOES AND MARRIAGE

Q. What do tornadoes and marriage have in common?

A. They both start with a lot of blowing and in the end you lose your house.

TURKEY SPERM

A woman has a new job collecting the sperm from turkeys to use for artificial insemination.

On the first day, as she approaches one turkey, it goes: 'Gobble gobble.'

She says, 'Quiet! You'll settle for a hand-job like the rest!'

TWO LESBIANS

Two lesbians are walking down the street with their hands down each other's knickers.

A man walks by and says, 'Why are you doing that?'

The first lesbian says, 'We're lip-reading.'

WHORES AND BITCHES

Q. What's the difference between a whore and a bitch?

A. A whore sleeps with everyone at a party and a bitch sleeps with everyone but you.

WIGAN WOMAN

Q. What's the difference between a woman from Wigan and a walrus?

A. One's got a moustache and smells of fish and the other lives in the sea.

WIVES AND JOBS

Q. What's the difference between your wife and your job?

A. After 10 years your job still sucks.

Ugly Wife

A husband and wife are getting ready for bed.

The wife is standing in front of a full-length mirror taking a long hard look at herself.

'You know, dear,' she says, 'I look in the mirror and I see an old woman. My face is wrinkled, my boobs barely clear my waist and my arse is sagging. I've got fat legs and my arms are flabby. Tell me something positive to make me feel better about myself.'

He says, 'Well, there's nothing wrong with your eyesight.'

WIVES AND VACUUM CLEANERS

Q. What do your wife and a vacuum cleaner have in common?
A. After a year they stop sucking and start whining.

WOMAN IN THE LIFT

A bloke walks into a lift and stands next to a beautiful woman.

After a few seconds he turns to her and says, 'Can I smell your knickers?'

The woman says, 'Certainly not!'

The man says, 'Hmm. It must be your feet, then.'

WOMAN'S DISAPPOINTMENT

A couple go to bed for the first time.

The woman says, 'Oh, dear, what a small organ.'

The bloke says, 'Well, I didn't think I'd be playing in the town hall.'

WOMAN'S FACE-LIFT

A woman in her late forties goes to a plastic surgeon for a face-lift.

The surgeon tells her about a new procedure called The Knob, in which a small knob is placed on the top of a woman's head and can be turned to tighten her skin, producing the effect of a face-lift.

She has the op. Over the next few years, she regularly

tightens her knob and stays youthful and pretty.

However, after 15 years she returns to the surgeon with two problems. She says, 'First, I have these terrible bags under my eyes and the knob won't get rid of them.'

The doctor says, 'Those aren't bags; those are your breasts.'

She says, 'Well, I suppose there's no point asking about the goatee.'

WOMAN'S HORMONES

A woman goes to her doctor to complain about the side-effects of the testosterone pills he'd given her.

She says, 'Doctor, I'm wondering if you got the dosage right. I've started growing hair in places I've never grown hair before.'

The doctor says, 'A little growth is a perfectly normal side-effect of testosterone. Just where has this happened?'

She says, 'On my balls.'

WOMAN'S PAINS

A woman visits her doctor to complain about strange abdominal pains.

He examines her and says, 'I hope you're looking forward to many sleepless nights because of crying and nappy-changing.'

'Why,' says the woman, 'am I pregnant?'

'No,' says the doctor, 'you've got bowel cancer.'

WOMAN STAYS QUIET

During sex, a bloke says to his wife, 'How come you never tell me when you have an orgasm?'

She says, 'You're never home.'

WOMAN'S WAIST

Q. Why is the space between a woman's breasts and hips called a waist?

A. Because you could fit another pair of tits there.

WOMAN'S WIND

A woman goes to her boyfriend's parents' house for dinner. This is her first time meeting the family and she's very nervous.

They all sit down and start to eat. The woman is beginning to feel a little discomfort, thanks to the broccoli casserole. The build-up of wind makes her eyes water. Left with no choice, she lets out a dainty little fart.

Hearing it, her boyfriend's father looks over at the family dog snoozing at the woman's feet and sternly says, 'Ginger!'

The woman smiles in relief.

A couple of minutes later, she feels the pain again. This time, she doesn't hesitate, and lets rip a much louder and longer fart.

The father again looks at the dog and yells, 'Damn it, Ginger!'

Again the woman smiles in relief.

A few minutes later, the woman has to fart once more. This time she doesn't even think about it, and lets rip with a fart that would rival a foghorn.

The father looks at the dog in disgust and yells, 'Damn it, Ginger, get away from her before she shits on you!'

WOMEN AND ALCOHOL

Q. Why was alcohol invented?

A. So ugly women could get laid.

GARY WAS DISAPPOINTED TO FIND
SHIRLEY'S REPUTATION AS A SLAPPER
WASN'T WHAT HE'D HOPED FOR

WOMEN AND CLOUDS

Q. What do women and clouds have in common?
A. Eventually they piss off and it's a nice day.

WOMEN AND COW PATS

Q. What do women and cow pats have in common?
A. The older they get, the easier they are to pick up.

WOMEN AND HURRICANES

Q. Why are hurricanes mostly named after women?
A. When they come they're wild and wet, but when they go they take your house and car.

WOMEN AND ORANGE JUICE

Q. Why are women like orange juice cartons?
A. It's not the size or shape that matters, or even how sweet the juice inside is: it's getting the bloody flaps open.

WOMEN AND PARKING SPACES

Q. Why are women like parking spaces?
A. All the good ones are taken and the ones left are handicapped.

WOMEN AND WASHING MACHINES

Q. What's the difference between a woman and a washing machine?
A. A washing machine doesn't expect you to ring after you've dumped your load in it.

WOMEN AND PIANOS

Q. Why are women like pianos?
A. When they're not upright, they're grand.

WOMEN AND ROTTWEILERS

Q. What's the difference between a woman with PMT and a rottweiler?
A. Lipstick.

WOMEN AND TERRORISTS

Q. What's the difference between a woman on her period and a terrorist?
A. You can negotiate with a terrorist.

WOMEN PLAYING GOLF

Two women are playing golf.

After hitting par on the first hole, they make their way to the second. Suddenly they hear a cry of 'Fore!', and one of the women gets hit on the head by a ball and collapses.

The second woman runs back to the clubhouse to get help.

She cries, 'My friend has been hit with a ball. Can someone come and look?'

The nearest bloke says, 'Sure, where was she hit?'

'Between the first and second holes.'

'Well, that doesn't leave much room for a plaster.'

WOMEN'S ORGASMS

Q. Why did God let women have orgasms?
A. It gives them another reason to moan.

WONDERBRA

Q. Why do they call it the Wonderbra?
A. Because when she takes it off, you wonder where her tits went.

CHAVS

CHAV AND A COCONUT

Q. What's the difference between a chav and a coconut?
A. One's thick and hairy, the other's a coconut.

CHAVS AT BEACHY HEAD

Q. Two chavs jump off Beachy Head. Who wins?
A. Society.

CHAV AT COLLEGE

Q. What do you call a chav at college?
A. The cleaner.

CHAV CROSSES ROAD

Q. Why did the chav cross the road?
A. To start a fight with a random stranger for no reason
   whatsoever.

CHAV ESKIMO

Q. What do you call an Eskimo chav?
A. An Innuinnit.

CHAV GIRL'S PROTECTION

Q. What does a chav girl use as protection during sex?
A. A bus shelter.

CHAV DEFINITION OF "DRESSING UP FOR A SPECIAL OCCASION"

CHAV HITS 30

Q. What do you call a 30-year-old chav girl?
A. Granny.

CHAV IN A BOX

Q. What do you call a chav in a box?
A. Innit.

CHAV IN A CABINET

Q. What do you call a chav in a filing cabinet?
A. Sorted.

CHAV IN A LOCKED BOX

Q. What do you call a chav in a box with a lock on it?
A. Safe.

CHAV IN A SUIT

Q. What do you say to a chav in a suit?
A. 'Will the defendant please stand?'

CHAV IN A TRACKSUIT

Q. What do you call a chav girl in a white tracksuit?
A. The bride.

CHAV ON A BIKE

Q. If you see a chav on a bike, why should you try not to hit him?
A. It might be your bike.

CHAV QUIZ NIGHT

Q. What's the first question at a chav quiz night?
A. 'What you lookin' at?'

CHAVS AND CLEANING

Q. How many chavs does it take to clean a floor?
A. None – dat's some uvver bleeder's job, innit?

CHAVS AND SLINKIES

Q. Why are chavs like Slinkies?
A. They have no real use but it's great to watch one fall down a flight of stairs.

CHAV'S FAVOURITE WINE

Q. What's a chav girl's favourite wine?
A. 'Aw, go on, take me to Lakeside, please, please, go on, take me...'

CHAVS IN A CAR

Q. Two chavs in a car without any music. Who's driving?
A. The police.

CHAVS IN A PHONE BOX

Q. How do you get 100 chavs into a phone box?
A. Paint three stripes on it.

CHAVS IN A RIVER

Q. What do you call 100 chavs at the bottom of a river?
A. A start.

Chav Wants a Job

A chav walks into the Jobcentre, marches up to the counter and says, 'Hi, I'm looking for a job.'

The man behind the counter replies, 'Well, we've just got a listing from a millionaire who wants a chauffeur/bodyguard for his nymphomaniac daughter. You'll have to drive around in a Mercedes, uniform provided. Because of the long hours, meals will be provided, and you'll also be required to escort the young lady on her holidays. The salary is £200k.'

The chav says, 'You're bullshitting me!'

The man says, 'Well, you started it!'

CHAV'S KNIFE

Q. What do you call a knife in a chav estate?
A. Exhibit A.

CHAV'S NIGHT OUT

Q. Where do you take a chav girl for a decent night out?
A. Up the arse.

CHAVS OVER A CLIFF

Q. Why is three chavs going over a cliff in a Nova a shame?
A. A Nova has four seats.

CHAV'S QUALIFICATIONS

Q. What do you call a chav with nine GCSEs?
A. A liar.

CHAVS' WELSH QUERY

Some chavs are driving through Wales.

As they approach Llanfairpwllgwyngyllgogerychwyrndrobwlll-antysiliogogogoch, they start arguing about the pronunciation of the town's name.

The row continues till lunchtime.

As they stand at the counter of the local restaurant, one chav says to the blonde serving girl, 'Before we order, could you settle an argument for us? Would you please pronounce where we are, very slowly?'

The blonde leans over the counter and says, 'Burrrrrrrrrgerrrrrrr Kiiiiing.'

CHAV TAKES A SHOWER

Q. Why did the chav take a shower?
A. He didn't mean to; he just forgot to close the Nova's window in the car wash.

CHAV WITH A JOB

Q. What do you say to a chav with a job?
A. 'A Big Mac, please.'

VIVE LA CHAV DIFFERENCE

Q. What's the difference between a chav girl and a chav bloke?
A. A chav girl has a higher sperm count.

CELEBRITIES

BEADLE'S PENIS

Jeremy Beadle has a small penis.
  But on the other hand, it's quite big.

BECKHAM AND AIRFIX

Q. What's the difference between David Beckham and an Airfix
  kit with no glue?
A. One's a glueless kit...

BECKHAM AND CHOCOLATE

Q. Why is David Beckham like a Ferrero Rocher?
A. They both come in a posh box.

BECKHAM AND POSH

Q. What's the difference between David Beckham and Posh?
A. Posh doesn't lash out when she's taken from behind.

BECKHAM AND SPERM

David Beckham walks into a sperm bank.

He says, 'I'd like to donate some sperm.'

The receptionist says, 'Certainly, sir. Have you donated before?'

Beckham says, 'Yes, you should have my details on your computer.'

The receptionist says, 'Ah, yes: I've found your profile, but I see you're going to need help. Shall I call Posh for you?'

Beckham says, 'Why do I need help?'

The receptionist says, 'It says on your profile that you're a useless wanker.'

"Paul McCartney's attracted some older visitors this year."

BECKHAM'S NEWS BET

Victoria and David Beckham are watching the Six O'Clock News.

The headline story is about a man who's threatening to jump off a bridge on to the busy road below.

Victoria turns to David and says, 'I bet you £10,000 that he jumps.'

David says, '£10,000? Done.'

The pair shake on it and continue watching.

Sure enough, the man jumps and hits the road below with a thud.

David takes £10,000 out of his pocket and gives it to Victoria.

Victoria says, 'I can't take that from you. I was cheating. I saw a news bulletin earlier, so I knew what was going to happen.'

David says, 'No, babe, the money's yours. I saw the earlier bulletin too; I just didn't think he'd do it again.'

BECKHAM'S SKINHEAD

Q. Why did David Beckham have a skinhead?

A. Because someone told Victoria sex would be better if she shaved her twat.

CAMILLA'S PAIN

Camilla goes to her doctor and says, 'When I suck Charles's dick, I get stomach ache.'

The doctor says, 'Have you tried Andrew's?'

CRUISE AND HOLMES

Tom Cruise has asked Kelly Holmes on a date.

He would've asked Paula Radcliffe but he wanted a girl who'd go all the way.

DOLLY'S KIDS

Q. How can you pick out Dolly Parton's kids in the playground?
A. They're the ones with stretch marks around their lips.

ENDLESS LOVE

Q. What's the definition of endless love?
A. Stevie Wonder and Ray Charles playing tennis.

GEORGE AND ELTON

George Michael and Elton John have written a gay version of
The Wizard of Oz.
   It's called Swallow the Yellow Thick Load.

GEORGE IN HOSPITAL

George Michael was rushed to hospital with a Mars bar in his
backside.
   Subsequent tests revealed it was actually a careless Wispa.

HEAD STUCK

Will Young, Robbie Williams and Kylie Minogue enjoy a night on
the town together.
   After they leave the nightclub, Kylie's drunkenly mucking
about when she gets her head stuck between some railings.
   Robbie decides to take full advantage of this and lifts up her
little skirt, pushes her thong to one side and gives her a good
seeing-to.

Robbie says, 'That was great. Your turn, Will!'
But Will is crying.
Robbie says, 'What's wrong, Will?'
Will sobs, 'My head won't fit between the railings.'

JACKO AND A BAG

Q. What's the difference between a supermarket bag and Michael Jackson?
A. One is white, made of plastic and should be kept away from small children. The other is used to hold your shopping.

JACKO AND ACNE

Q. What's the difference between Michael Jackson and acne?
A. Acne doesn't come on your face until you're fifteen.

JACKO AND HOMEWORK

Q. What do Michael Jackson and homework have in common?
A. They're a pain in the arse to kids.

JACKO AND WIFE

Michael Jackson and his wife are in the recovery room with their new baby son.

The doctor walks in and Michael says, 'Doctor, how long before we can have sex?'

The doctor says, 'I'd wait until he's at least 14.'

JACKO DROWNING

Q. What did Michael Jackson shout when he was drowning?
A. 'Throw me a buoy!'

JACKO RACE

Q. Why can you always win a race with Michael Jackson?
A. Because he likes to come in a little behind.

JACKO RAID

The FBI have raided Michael Jackson's house.

They found class A drugs in his kitchen, class B drugs in his living room and Class 5C in his bedroom.

JACKO'S BEDTIME

Q. How do you know when it's bedtime at the Neverland Ranch?
A. When the big hand touches the little hand.

JACKO'S NIGHT IN

Janet and Michael Jackson are at home one night.
  Janet says, 'Shall we get a pizza and a video?'
  Michael says, 'Sure. Can we get Aladdin?'
  Janet says, 'No; just a pizza and a video.'

JACKO'S PANTS

Q. Why are Michael Jackson's pants so small?
A. Because they aren't his.

JAMIE AND A RUN

Q. What's the difference between Jamie Oliver and a marathon?
A. One's a pant in the country...

KING'S KIDS

Q. Which king has had the most children?
A. Jonathan.

LESLIE CRIES

Q. Why does John Leslie cry during sex?
A. Pepper spray.

Proof of Identity

St Peter is standing guard over Heaven when a man approaches, claiming to be Bill Gates.

St Peter asks for proof of identity, so Bill shows his bank balance.

St Peter says, 'In you go.'

A second man approaches, claiming to be Stephen Hawking. St Peter asks for proof of identity, so Hawking explains the Big Bang Theory.

St Peter says, 'In you go.'

A third man approaches, claiming to be David Beckham. But when St Peter asks him to prove his identity, Beckham gets annoyed.

St Peter says, 'Come on. Even Bill Gates and Stephen Hawking had to do it.'

Beckham says, 'Who?'

St Peter says, 'In you go.'

NEW SITCOM

Q. Heard about Michael Barrymore's new sitcom?
A. It's called Only Pools and Corpses.

NO ASHTRAYS

Q. Why doesn't Michael Barrymore keep any ashtrays in the house?
A. Because he puts the fags out in the swimming pool.

PETE AND BILL

Q. What do you get if you cross Pete Doherty with Bill Oddie?
A. A quack addict.

QUEEN'S GIFT

Q. What did the Queen buy Camilla for her wedding
  anniversary?
A. A weekend in Paris and a chauffeur-driven Mercedes.

ROCK PARTY

It's the Sixties, and one night Michael Caine throws a party for
all his favourite bands: Led Zeppelin, Deep Purple, the Doors,
the Rolling Stones, the Beatles and loads more, together with
models, film stars and loads of groupies.

For his special favourites, The Doors, he's arranged a special
treat. He gathers the band together and says, 'See that yellow
door at the end of the corridor? There's a girl in there waiting
for you and she wants to suck off all four of you.'

Jim Morrison and the guys are excited and charge off to the
yellow room. Sure enough, there's a very sexy, very naked rock
chick there, and she does indeed proceed to blow all four of
them, one at a time.

They rejoin the party satisfied, and Jim tells Mick Jagger
what a great time they had. Next thing you know, Mick and the
rest of the Rolling Stones pile into the yellow room and the
groupie starts to give them the same treatment.

Five minutes later, as she's working on Keith Richards, in
bursts Michael Caine.

'What the hell are you doing, girl?' he cries. 'You were only
supposed to blow the bloody Doors off!'

ROD HULL, R.I.P.

Q. Did you go to Rod Hull's funeral?
A. Apparently the reception was crap.

SWALLOWED A CONDOM

Victoria Beckham phones the doctor in a panic late one night.
    She says, 'Doctor, you've got to come over. David's just swallowed a condom.'
    The doctor rushes to get his things together when the phone rings. It's Victoria again.
    She says, 'Don't worry, Doc, there's no need to come round. We've found another one.'

THREE LEGS

Q. What's got three legs and lives on a farm?
A. The McCartney family.

TOMMY COOPER, R.I.P.

Q. How did Tommy Cooper die?
A. Just like that.

TOP OF THE STAIRS

Q. What's black and sits at the top of the stairs?
A. Stephen Hawking in a house fire.

UGLIEST IN THE LAND

Snow White, Tom Thumb and Quasimodo are sitting in a pub with their mates.

Snow White says, 'There's no doubt about it: I'm the fairest in the land.'

Tom Thumb says, 'There's no doubt about it: I'm the smallest in the land.'

Quasimodo says, 'There's no doubt about it: I'm the ugliest in the land.'

Their mates tell them to prove it by going to the magic all-knowing mirror.

The three head off.

A few minutes later, the door of the pub bursts open and Snow White runs in and shouts, 'It's official – I'm the fairest in the land!'

Shortly afterwards, the door again bursts open and Tom Thumb runs in and shouts, 'It's official – I'm the smallest in the land!'

Five minutes later, the door gets kicked in and Quasimodo stomps through and bellows, 'Who the hell is Jade Goody?'

WONDER'S WIFE

Q. Have you seen Stevie Wonder's wife lately?
A. Neither has he.

FOOTBALL

ABERDEEN FAN AND THE SHEEP

An Aberdeen fan is trapped on a desert island, alone apart from a sheep and a dog.

Soon, the sheep looks very attractive to the Aberdeen fan.

The problem is that whenever he approaches the sheep, the dog growls threateningly.

The Aberdeen fan takes the dog to the opposite side of the island, giving it some food as a distraction. He runs back to the sheep, only to find the dog has made it back first, and is growling at him.

Next, the Aberdeen fan ties the dog to a tree with a large leash. He goes back to the sheep, only to find the dog growling with a gnawed-off leash round its neck.

The Aberdeen fan is getting more and more sexually frustrated.

But as he sits under a palm tree staring out to sea, a beautiful woman in a sexy bikini emerges from the surf.

She asks him who he is and, taking pity on him, asks if there's anything she can do tonight to stop him feeling lonely.

The Aberdeen fan thinks for a moment and says, 'Could you take the dog for a walk?'

ARSENAL FANS SMELL

Q. Why do Arsenal fans smell?
A. So the blind can hate them as well.

BIRMINGHAM FAN'S GRENADE

Q. What should you do if a Birmingham fan throws a grenade at you?
A. Pull the pin out and throw it back.

CELTIC VAN DRIVER

A Celtic-supporting van driver used to keep himself amused by scaring every Rangers fan he saw sauntering down the street.

He would swerve as if to hit them, and at the last minute, swerve back on to the road.

One day, as he was driving, he saw a priest hitch-hiking. He thought he would do his good deed for the day and offer the priest a lift.

The driver says, 'Where are you off to, Father?'

The priest says, 'I'm going to give Mass at St Michael's Church. It's about two miles down the road.'

The driver says, 'No problem. Jump in.'

The priest climbs aboard and they set off.

Suddenly the driver sees a Rangers fan walking along the pavement, and instinctively swerves as if to hit him. But just in time he remembers there's a priest in his van, so swerves back on to the road again, narrowly missing the Rangers fan.

However, although he's sure he didn't hit him, he still hears a loud thud.

Wondering where the noise came from, he glances in his

mirrors and, seeing nothing, says to the priest, 'I'm worried, Father. I just missed that Rangers fan who was walking down the road.'

The priest says, 'No need to worry. I got the bastard with the door.'

CHELSEA WHISTLE

Q. Why do Chelsea fans whistle while they're sitting on the toilet?

A. So they know which end to wipe.

Charlton Suicide

A man distraught about Charlton's poor form prepares to hang himself.

He decides to wear his full Charlton kit.

A neighbour discovers the body and tells a policeman.

On arrival, the policeman quickly removes the dead man's Charlton kit and dresses the man in stockings and suspenders.

Baffled, the neighbour asks why.

The policeman says, 'It's to avoid embarrassing the family.'

CORPSE'S CORK

An Evertonian undertaker takes on an apprentice.

The apprentice walks up to his first corpse and examines it. He rolls it over and is amazed to find a cork stuck in the corpse's arsehole.

Mystified, he pulls it out and hears the strains of You'll Never Walk Alone coming out.

Startled, he shoves the cork back in and runs off to find his boss.

He says, 'You've got to come and help me. I've just found a cork in one of the corpse's arseholes, and you won't believe what happens when you pull it out!'

The old undertaker follows his assistant, and is mildly surprised to see that there is indeed a cork plugging the body's back door.

He pulls it out, and again, the strains of You'll Never Walk Alone can be heard emanating from the orifice.

The undertaker turns to his assistant and says, 'What's so surprising? You can hear 40,000 arseholes singing that every other Saturday.'

DAD'S JOB

A teacher asks all the children what their dads do for a living.

All the usual answers come up: salesman, builder, fireman and so on.

But little Johnny doesn't raise his hand.

The teacher says, 'Come on, Johnny. We want to know what your dad does.'

Johnny says, 'My dad is an exotic dancer in a gay club and takes off all his clothes in front of other men. Sometimes, if the offer's really good, he goes out with a man, rents a cheap hotel room and lets them sleep with him.'

The teacher quickly sets the other children some work and takes little Johnny aside to ask him if that was really true.

Johnny says, 'No, he plays football for Scotland, but I was too embarrassed to say.'

DEAD DOG

Q. What's the difference between a dead dog in the road and a
dead Manchester United fan in the road?
A. The dog has skid marks in front of it.

Kelly

i'd watch this ref, he loves dishing out punishment.

EVERTON SEASON TICKET

Two Everton fans are in a pub.

The first one says, 'I was so pissed off with the team the other day that I nailed my season ticket to the club gates.'

The second one says, 'But that's money down the drain.'

The first one says, 'I know, so the next day I went back for it – only to find some bastard had nicked my nail.'

FARTBALL

An old man and his wife are in bed.

After lying there for a few minutes, the old man farts and shouts, 'Goal!'

His wife says, 'What the hell was that?'

The old man says, 'I'm ahead one-nil.'

A few minutes later, the wife lets one go and shouts, 'Goal! One-all!'

After another ten minutes, the old man farts again. 'Goal! Two-one!'

The wife quickly farts again and shouts, 'Goal! Two-all!'

Not to be outdone, the old man strains as hard as he can to squeeze out the winning fart.

Unfortunately, he tries too hard and shits the bed.

His wife says, 'What the hell was that?'

The old man says, 'Half-time. Swap sides...'

FIGHTING DOCTORS

A nurse is walking through the hospital when she sees two doctors fighting.

She breaks them up and yells, 'Why are you fighting?'

The first doctor says, 'It's that man on E Ward – you know,

the one with the Manchester United pyjamas. Dr Jones here
has just told him that he's only got two weeks left to live.'

The nurse says, 'Look, Dr Smith. There was really nothing
more we could do for the man – he just had to be told.'

The first doctor says, 'I know that, but I wanted to be the one
who got to tell the bastard.'

FOUR SURGEONS

Four surgeons are taking a tea break.

The first surgeon says, 'Accountants are the best to operate
on, because when you open them up, everything inside is
numbered.'

The second surgeon says, 'No, librarians are the best.
Everything inside them is in alphabetical order.'

The third surgeon says, 'You should try electricians.
Everything inside them is colour-coded.'

The fourth surgeon says, 'I prefer Tottenham fans. They're
heartless, spineless, gutless and their heads and arses are
interchangeable.'

GLORY, GLORY

A woman visits her doctor and says, 'I keep hearing the sound
of "Glory, glory Man United" coming from my crotch!'

The doctor says, 'Don't worry, a lot of twats sing that.'

JAMES' SUICIDE BID

David James is so despondent after his latest blunder he
decides to end it all, so he throws himself down in front of a
number 57 bus.

Luckily, it passes under him.

KEWELL AND DIOUF

Did you hear that Harry Kewell and El Hadji Diouf have formed a superhero partnership?

They're calling themselves Crapman and Gobbin'.

KOSOVO SIGNING

Liverpool sign a player from Kosovo.

On his debut he scores a hat-trick as Liverpool come from two down to win.

After the game, he calls home and tells his mother what an amazing day he's had.

She says, 'I'm so pleased for you, but things aren't so great over here. Today, dad's been shot, I got beaten and robbed and your sister's been raped.'

The player says, 'That's terrible, mum. But you understand that it was for the good of all of us that I left home and came to Liverpool, don't you?'

His mum says, 'Of course, but did you have to bring us with you?'

LEEDS FANS' SKY-DIVE

Q. What do you call 20 Leeds fans sky-diving?
A. Diarrhoea.

LIVERPOOL CLASS

A teacher starts a new job at a school on Merseyside and, trying to make a good impression on her first day, explains to her class that she is a Liverpool fan.

She asks her students to raise their hands if they, too, are Liverpool fans.

Everyone in the class raises their hand except one little girl.

The teacher looks at her and says, 'Mary, why didn't you raise your hand?'

Mary says, 'Because I'm not a Liverpool fan.'

The teacher says, 'If you're not a Liverpool fan, who are you a fan of?'

Mary says, 'I'm a Manchester United fan.'

The teacher says, 'Why?'

Mary says, 'Because my mum is a United fan and my dad is a United fan, so I'm a United fan, too.'

The teacher says, 'That's no reason for you to be a United fan. You don't have to be just like your parents all the time. What if your mum was a prostitute and your dad was a drug addict – what would you be then?'

Mary says, 'A Liverpool fan.'

"During these qualifiers there's to be no late nights and no sex...not even with your wives."

MAN UTD BIRTH CONTROL

Q. What do United fans use as birth control?
A. Their personalities.

MAN UTD FAN AND VIBRATOR

Q. What's the difference between a Manchester United fan and a vibrator?
A. A Manchester United fan is a real dick.

MAN UTD FAN IN HEAVEN

A Manchester United fan dies on match day and goes to heaven wearing his Manchester United shirt.

He knocks on the pearly gates and out walks St Peter.

St Peter says, 'Sorry, no Manchester United fans allowed in Heaven.'

Astounded, the Manchester United fan says, 'But I've been a good man!'

St Peter says, 'Oh, really? What have you done?'

The Manchester United fan says, 'Three weeks before I died, I gave £10 to Save the Children.'

St Peter says, 'Hmm. Anything else?'

The Manchester United fan says, 'Two weeks before I died, I gave £10 to the homeless.'

St Peter says, 'Hmm. Anything else?'

The Manchester United fan says, 'A week before I died, I gave £10 to the Albanian orphans.'

St Peter says, 'Very well. Wait here a minute while I have a word with the boss.'

Two minutes later, St Peter returns.

He says, 'I've had a word with God and he agrees with me. Here's your £30 back; now fuck off.'

MAN UTD STAMPS

The Post Office has recalled its Manchester United-themed stamps.

People couldn't work out which side to spit on.

MIDDLESBROUGH PITCH

They say the Riverside Stadium has the best pitch in the Premiership.

Not surprising, when you think of all the shit that's been on it.

MILLWALL FAN AND ONION

Q. What's the difference between a Millwall fan and an onion?
A. No one would cry if you chopped up a Millwall fan.

NEWCASTLE BUS

Q. What's the difference between a porcupine and the Newcastle team bus?
A. The porcupine has pricks on the outside.

Newcastle Transfer

David Beckham has turned down a move to Newcastle United.

Real Madrid and Newcastle had agreed a £15 million transfer fee for the England star.

But Beckham said there was no way he could join Newcastle after what the Toon Army had done to Thailand.

NORWICH FAN'S GIRLFRIEND

Q. What do you call a Norwich fan with a girlfriend?
A. A shepherd.

ONE-MAN TEAM

Before a friendly between England and Scotland, Wayne Rooney walks into the dressing room to discover that half the team is asleep.

Rooney says, 'What's going on?'

David Beckham says, 'We just can't motivate ourselves, because it's only Scotland.'

Rooney says, 'Tell you what, lads, why don't you have a rest down the pub, and I'll face them myself?'

So the team goes to the pub.

After a while, they wonder how the match is going and get the landlord to put the match on TV.

The scoreline at the top of the screen says, 'England 1 Scotland 0: Wayne Rooney, 10 minutes.' The players cheer, then turn the telly off and return to their drinks.

After a while, Rio Ferdinand says, 'It'll be full time now. Let's see how Wayne got on.'

The final score comes up as, 'England 1 Scotland 1: Barry Ferguson, 89 minutes.'

The England players rush to the stadium to congratulate Rooney.

However, they find him crying.

Rooney says, 'I'm really sorry, lads – I let you down.'

Beckham says, 'Don't be daft. You drew with Scotland all on your own!'

Rooney says, 'But I'm so ashamed: I got sent off in the 12th minute.'

OWEN ON THE PULL

Michael Owen walks into a nightclub, goes straight up to a girl, starts feeling her tits and says, 'Get your coat, sexy, you're coming home with me.'

The girl says, 'You're a little forward.'

PALACE FAN DRINKING

Q. How do you kill a Palace fan while he's drinking?
A. Slam the toilet seat on his head.

PAVE A DRIVEWAY

Q. How many Manchester United fans does it take to pave a driveway?
A. Depends how thin you slice them.

POOR OLD EMILE

After a disastrous match, Sven Goran Eriksson yells, 'Heskey, you were crap.'

David Beckham, trying to reassure his team-mate, says, 'Don't listen to him, Emile. He doesn't know what he's talking about. He just repeats what everybody else says.'

PREGNANCY QUERY

A woman goes to her doctor and says, 'Can you get pregnant from anal sex?'

The doctor says, 'Of course. Where do you think Leicester fans come from?'

RIO'S GRAN

Rio Ferdinand goes to the doctor.

The doctor says, 'I've got some bad news and some good news for you.'

Rio says, 'What is it?'

The doctor says, 'The bad news is your grandmother has died.'

Rio says, 'Oh my God, no! What's the good news?'

The doctor says, 'Wayne Rooney can't shag her now.'

ROONEY AND THE DOCTOR

Wayne Rooney goes to the doctor and says, 'I don't understand it. Every time I look in the mirror, I become sexually excited.'

The doctor says, 'That's because you look like a twat.'

ROONEY'S FEAT

Q. How does Wayne Rooney hit two balls at the same time?
A. By stepping on a rake.

SEVEN DWARVES

The seven dwarves are in a cave when suddenly it collapses.

Snow White is frightened for their lives, until she hears a voice from inside the cave saying, 'Middlesbrough are good enough to qualify for the Champions League.'

She says, 'Thank Christ; at least Dopey's all right.'

SUPPORTERS' HATS

Three football fans are walking home when they see a naked woman lying dead in the middle of the street.

After they call the police, they each take off their hats and place them on the dead woman to cover her up until the cops arrive. The first fan places his Spurs hat over her left breast, the second places his Chelsea hat over her right breast, and the third fan places his Arsenal hat over her crotch.

The policeman arrives and examines the body.

He lifts the Spurs hat and quickly replaces it. Then he lifts the Chelsea cap and quickly replaces it.

However, when he lifts the Arsenal hat, he stares for what feels like ages.

Finally, he lets the hat drop and turns to walk away.

The fans are curious, and ask him why he spent so much time inspecting the woman's vagina.

The policeman says, 'It's the first time I've seen anything other than an arsehole under an Arsenal hat.'

SVEN'S RAGE

Sven Goran Eriksson spots a turd on England's training pitch.

He shouts, 'Who's shit on the ground?'

Emile Heskey says, 'I am, boss, but I'm OK in the air.'

"The detail's brilliant! Beckham's got a mobile in each hand and a raging hard-on."

SWEARING NAMES

Q. Which are the three English teams with swear words in their name?
A. Arse-nal, S-cunt-horpe and Manchester fucking United.

THREE FEET LONG

Q. What's three feet long and keeps a twat warm?
A. A Manchester United scarf.

TOON FANS AND LAXATIVES

Q. What do Newcastle fans and laxatives have in common?
A. Both irritate the crap out of you.

TWO BULLETS

You're trapped in a room with a tiger, a rattlesnake and an Arsenal fan. You have a gun with two bullets. What should you do?

Shoot the Arsenal fan twice.

WHISTLES AND LICKS

Q. What whistles and licks Sir Alex Ferguson's arse?
A. A Premiership ref.

IN THE NEWS

BLAIR AND THE PIG

Tony Blair and his driver are on their way to Chequers and pass a farm.

Suddenly, a pig jumps out into the middle of the road.

The driver tries to swerve out of the way, but hits him.

He goes to the farmhouse to explain what's happened.

Ten minutes later, he returns to the car holding a beer and a cigar.

Blair notices this and says, 'What on earth did you tell them?'

The driver says, 'I told them that I'm Tony Blair's driver and I just killed the pig.'

BLAIR SAVED

Tony Blair is out jogging and accidentally falls into a very cold river.

Three boys see the accident.

Without a second thought, they jump into the water and drag out the soaking Blair.

Blair says, 'Boys, you saved my life and deserve a reward. You name it; I'll give it to you.'

The first boy says, 'I'd like a ticket to Disneyland.'

Blair says, 'Certainly.'

The second boy says, 'I'd like an MP3 player.'

Blair says, 'No problem.'

The third boy says, 'And I'd like a wheelchair with a stereo in it.'

Blair says, 'But you're not handicapped.'

The boy says, 'No, but I will be when my dad finds out I saved you from drowning.'

BLAIR'S ORDER

Tony and Cherie Blair are at a restaurant.

The waiter tells them that tonight's special is chicken amandine and fresh fish.

Cherie says, 'The chicken sounds good; I'll have that.'

The waiter says, 'Certainly, madam. And the vegetable?'

Cherie says, 'Oh, he'll have the fish.'

BUSH IN HELL

George W Bush has a heart attack and dies. He immediately goes to Hell, where the Devil is waiting for him.

The Devil says, 'I don't know what to do. You're on my list, but I have no room for you. Tell you what: I've got some people here who weren't quite as bad as you. I'll let one of them go, but you have to take their place. I'll even let you decide who you swap with.'

The Devil leads Bush to a series of doors and opens the first. Inside is Ronald Reagan and a large pool of water. Reagan keeps diving in and surfacing, over and over again. Such is his fate in Hell.

Bush says, 'No, I don't want to do that. I'm not a good swimmer, so I don't think I could do that all day long.'

The Devil leads him to the next room. Inside is Richard Nixon with a sledgehammer and a huge pile of rocks. All he does is swing the hammer, time after time after time.

Bush says, 'No; I've got a problem with my shoulder. I'd be in constant agony if all I did was break rocks all day.'

The Devil opens a third door. Inside, Bush sees Bill Clinton, lying on the floor with his arms tied behind his head, and his legs spreadeagled. Bent over him is Monica Lewinsky, doing what she does best.

Bush stares in disbelief and says, 'Yeah, I can handle this.'

The Devil smiles and says, 'OK, Monica, you're free to go.'

BUSH'S BLINDFOLD

On his birthday, George W Bush comes down to breakfast to find his wife holding a blindfold.

She says she has a surprise and blindfolds him. She sits him in a chair at the kitchen table, just as a man tells her she has a call. She tells Bush not to take off the blindfold, as she'll be right back.

As Bush is waiting, and since his wife isn't there to see him, he decides to masturbate to pass the time.

He pulls down his pants and starts jerking off. He moans in pleasure and makes other noises, but his wife doesn't hear him. Then he hears his wife's footsteps approaching.

He tucks his cock into his pants and wipes his hands on his trousers, just before she enters the room.

His wife says, 'OK, you can take your blindfold off.'

Bush takes the blindfold off and sees a group of people at the table.

His wife says, 'The networks are filming your birthday, live on every channel!'

BUSH'S BURGER

George W Bush strides into a library and shouts, 'Hi, ma'am! I'd like a burger and fries please!'

The librarian says, 'For fuck's sake, you idiot, this is a library!'

'Sorry,' says Bush, and whispers, 'I'd like a burger and fries, please.'

BUSH'S WAR PLANS

A bloke walks into a bar and says to the bartender, 'Isn't that George W Bush and Colin Powell sitting over there?'

The bartender says, 'Yep, that's them.'

So the bloke walks over to them and says, 'Wow, this is a real honour. What are you guys doing in here?'

Bush says, 'We're planning World War Three.'

The bloke says, 'Really? What's going to happen?'

Bush says, 'Well, this time we're going to kill 50 million Arabs and one bicycle repairman.'

The bloke cries, 'A bicycle repairman? Why kill a bicycle repairman?'

Bush turns to Powell and says, 'See, dummy! I told you no one would worry about the 50 million Arabs!'

"They just don't understand country ways.
Next they'll ban us from sleeping with our sisters!"

Donations for Brown

A bloke is driving home from work and notices there is a lot more traffic than normal.

Eventually, all the cars grind to a halt. He sees a policeman walking towards his car, so he asks him what's wrong.

The policeman says, 'It's a crisis. Gordon Brown is sitting in the road very upset. He doesn't have the £10 billion needed to fill the black hole in his budget, and everyone hates him. He's threatening to douse himself in petrol and set himself on fire.'

The bloke says, 'What are you doing about it?'

The policeman says, 'I'm going car-to-car asking for donations.'

The man says, 'How much do you have so far?'

The policeman says, 'So far, only 99 litres, but a lot of people are still siphoning as we speak.'

CHARLES' WISH

Prince Charles is driving around the Queen's estate when he accidentally runs over her favourite corgi.

He gets out of his car and sit down on the grass, distraught. His mother will be furious.

Suddenly, he notices a lamp half-buried in the ground.

He digs it up, polishes it and immediately a genie appears.

The genie says, 'You have freed me from thousands of years of imprisonment. As a reward, I shall grant you one wish.'

Charles says, 'I have all the material things I need, but do you think you could bring this dog back to life?'

The genie looks at the splattered remains and shakes his head.

He says, 'You ask too much. The body is too far gone. Its bones are crushed and its brains are splashed all over the road. Even I couldn't bring it back to life. Is there something else you'd like?'

Charles reaches into his pocket and pulls out two photos.

He shows the genie the first photo and says, 'I was married to this beautiful woman called Diana.'

Then he shows the genie the second photo and says, 'But now I'm married to this woman called Camilla. Do you think you can make her as beautiful as Diana?'

The genie studies the two photographs and says, 'Let's have another look at that dog.'

CONDOM EMBLEM

The government today announced that it's changing its emblem to a condom because it more accurately reflects its political stance.

A condom allows for inflation, halts production, destroys the next generation, protects a bunch of pricks and gives you a sense of security while you're actually being screwed.

CREMATED POPE

Q. Why was John Paul II cremated?
A. Because the Vatican wanted to use his ashes as Pope-
pourri.

FIRING SQUAD

Tony Blair, Jacques Chirac and George W Bush are set to face
a firing squad in a small Central American country.

Blair is the first one placed against the wall, but he has a
cunning plan.

Just before the order to shoot is given, he yells,
'Earthquake!'

The firing squad looks round in a panic, while Blair vaults
over the wall and escapes.

Chirac is the second one placed against the wall.

The squad is reassembled, but Chirac has been inspired by
Blair's getaway.

So before the order to shoot is given, Chirac yells, 'Tornado!'

Again the squad is distracted, and Chirac escapes over the
wall.

Finally, Bush is placed against the wall.

He thinks, 'I see the pattern here. You just scream out
something to alarm everyone, then hop over the wall.'

So as the rifles are raised in his direction, Bush grins from
ear to ear and yells, 'Fire!'

FOOTBALLING ARAFAT

After Yassar Arafat died, the Palestinian undertakers clothed
his body in a Newcastle shirt, Spurs shorts and Rangers socks.

In his will he'd said he wanted to be buried in the Gaza strip.

GOLD URINAL

Before his inauguration, George W Bush was invited on a tour of the White House by his predecessor Bill Clinton.

After drinking several glasses of iced tea, he asked Clinton if he could use his personal bathroom.

Once inside, he was astonished to see that Clinton had a solid gold urinal.

That afternoon, Bush told his wife Laura about the urinal.

He said, 'Just think. When I'm President, I'll have my own personal gold urinal.'

Later, when Laura had lunch with Hillary Clinton, she told her how impressed George had been by the fact that Bill had a gold urinal.

That evening, Bill and Hillary were getting ready for bed.

Hillary said, 'Well, I found out who pissed in your saxophone.'

INFLATABLE DOLL

A bloke goes into a sex shop and asks for an inflatable doll.

The man behind the counter says, 'Normal or Palestinian?'

The customer says, 'What's the difference?'

The man behind the counter says, 'The Palestinian one blows itself up.'

LABOUR BRAIN OP

An office worker is so frustrated at being passed over for promotion year after year that he goes to a brain-transplant centre in the hope of adding 20 points to his IQ.

The surgeon says, 'This is an expensive operation. An ounce of doctor's brain, for example, costs £1,000. An ounce of accountant's brain costs £2,000. An ounce of lawyer's brain is £50,000. And an ounce of Labour MP's brain is £100,000.'

The office worker says, 'All that money, just for an ounce of Labour MP's brain? Why on earth is that?'

The surgeon says, 'Do you have any idea how many Labour MPs we would have to kill?'

LAURA ON TOP

Q. Why does Laura Bush have to go on top?
A. Because George W Bush always fucks up.

LIE CLOCKS

A man dies and goes to heaven.

As he stands in front of St Peter at the Pearly Gates, he sees a huge wall of clocks behind him.

He says, 'What are all those clocks?'

St Peter says, 'Those are Lie Clocks. Everyone on Earth has a Lie Clock. Every time you lie, the hands on your clock will move.'

The man says, 'Oh. Whose clock is that?'

St Peter says, 'That's Mother Teresa's. The hands never moved, indicating that she never told a lie.'

The man says, 'Incredible. And whose clock is that one?'

St Peter says, 'That's Abraham Lincoln's clock. The hands moved twice, telling us that Lincoln told only two lies in his entire life.'

The man says, 'Where's George W Bush's clock?'

St Peter says, 'In Jesus's office. He's using it as a ceiling fan.'

PARACHUTES

George W Bush, the Pope and a little boy are on the same plane.

Suddenly the engines fail and the captain says, 'We're going to crash. Grab a parachute and escape while you can.'

The three of them rush over to the parachutes – but find there are only two.

Bush grabs one, opens the door and jumps out, shouting, 'I'm too important to die!'

The Pope and the little boy look at each other.

The Pope says, 'Little boy, I've had a good long life and I'm sure I'll be going to a better place. You take the parachute.'

The little boy says, 'It's OK, you have it – and I'll have the second one. That tit Bush took my rucksack.'

PRESCOTT'S CRASH

John Prescott crashes his car into a lamp-post.

A paramedic rushes to the scene and says, 'Where are you bleeding from?'

Prescott says, 'Hull.'

ROYAL HONEYMOON

At the Royal wedding, Camilla was in agony: her shoes were way too small.

When she and Charles got to the bridal suite, the only thing she could think of was getting her shoes off.

The rest of the Royal Family crowded round the bedroom door and heard what they expected: grunts and straining noises.

Eventually they heard Charles say, 'My, that was tight.'

The Queen whispered, 'Told you Camilla was a virgin.'

Then, to their surprise, they heard Charles say, 'Right. Now for the other one.'

There followed more grunting, until Charles said, 'My God! That was even tighter!'

'That's my boy,' said the Duke. 'Once a sailor, always a sailor!'

QUEEN'S HOSPITAL VISIT

The Queen is visiting one of London's top hospitals and she says she wants to see absolutely everything.

During her tour, she passes a room where a male patient is masturbating.

The Queen says, 'Oh my, that's disgraceful. What's the meaning of this?'

The doctor leading the tour says, 'I'm sorry, your Majesty, but this man has a very serious medical condition and is only following doctor's orders. His body produces too much semen and his testicles keep overfilling. Until we can find out exactly what's causing this problem, he's been instructed to do this at least five times a day or there's a danger that his testicles will explode, killing him instantly.'

The Queen says, 'Oh, I am sorry.'

On the next floor, they pass a room where a young nurse is giving a patient a blow-job.

The Queen says, 'Oh my, what's happening in there?'

The doctor says, 'Same problem, but he's with BUPA.'

SEX AND DRIVING LESSONS

Q. Why doesn't Osama Bin Laden have sex and driving lessons on the same day?

A. The camel can't manage it.

SHIPMAN SUICIDE

Harold Shipman died after being found hanged in his cell.

A prison spokesman said that the killer doctor had simply run out of patients.

SMART PEOPLE

While having tea with the Queen, George W Bush asks how she makes sure she's surrounded by smart people.

She says, 'I ask the right questions.'

With that, she phones Tony Blair and says, 'Please answer this riddle: your mother has a child, and your father has a child, and the child is not your brother or your sister. Who is it?'

Tony Blair says, 'It's me, ma'am.'

Bush, impressed, returns to Washington and summons Dick Cheney.

Bush says, 'Your mother has a child, and your father has a child, and the child is not your brother or your sister. Who is it?'

A puzzled Cheney says, 'Can I get back to you?'

In desperation, he calls Condoleeza Rice for help.

She immediately answers, 'It's me, of course.'

Cheney rushes back to the White House, finds Bush, and says, 'I know the answer, sir! I know who it is! It's Condoleeza Rice!'

Bush says in disgust, 'Wrong, you dumb shit; it's Tony Blair!'

TERRORIST DRINK

Q. What's al-Qaeda's favourite drink?
A. Osama Bin Latte.

TRAGEDY

George W Bush visits a school to deliver a basic talk on Greek literature.

He sits in front of the class and says, 'Who knows what a tragedy is?'

A small boy says, 'Say my friend got run over by a tractor and died. Would that be a tragedy?'

Bush says, 'No, that's not a tragedy – that would be an accident.'

A small girl says, 'Is it when a bus of little children crashes and they die?'

Bush says, 'No, but it would be a great loss.'

Another boy says, 'Would a tragedy be if Air Force One was shot down and you died?'

Bush says, 'Why do you say that?'

The boy says, 'Because it wouldn't be an accident and it certainly wouldn't be a great loss.'

TWELVE INCHES

Q. What's 12 inches long and dangles in front of an arsehole?
A. Tony Blair's tie.

UKRAINE Y-FRONTS

Q. Why shouldn't you wear Y-fronts in Ukraine?
A. Chernobyl fallout.

"Apparently, one of the drugs the Greek weightlifter tested positive for was Viagra."

X-RATED

ADOLESCENT RABBIT

Q. What do you call an adolescent rabbit?
A. A pubic hare.

BABIES

Q. How many babies does it take to paint a wall?
A. Depends how hard you throw them.

BAKER'S HANDS

Q. Why did the baker have smelly hands?
A. He kneaded a crap.

BEES' MILK

Q. What bees make milk?
A. Boo-bees.

BEREFT DRUNK

A drunk is staggering down the street with his car keys in his hand and his cock hanging out when he sees a policeman.

He points at his keys and says, 'Officer, somebody's stolen my car.'

The policeman says, 'Where did you last see it?'

The drunk says, 'On the end of this key.'

The policeman notices that the drunk's cock is hanging out and says, 'Sir, are you aware that you're exposing yourself?'

The drunk looks down and cries, 'Oh no, they got my girlfriend too!'

BIGGEST DRAWBACK

Q. What's the biggest drawback in the jungle?
A. An elephant's foreskin.

BLIND FOOTBALL

A coach of blind kids are on a day trip when the driver feels thirsty. He spots a pub and pulls up.

He says, 'Time for a break. Here's a field – what would you like to do?'

One boy says they'd like to play football.

The driver says, 'But you're blind. Are you able to play?'

The boy says, 'Yes, we've got a special ball that has a bell in so we can follow it.'

So the driver goes to the pub. A while later, a policeman bursts through the pub door and yells, 'Who's in charge of those blind kids?'

The driver says, 'They're not causing trouble, are they?'

The policeman says, 'Trouble? They've just kicked a Morris dancer to death.'

BLONDE, BRUNETTE, BLONDE

Q. What is blonde, brunette, blonde, brunette, blonde?
A. A blonde doing cartwheels.

BLUE AND ORANGE

Q. What's blue and orange and lies at the bottom of a swimming pool?
A. A baby with burst armbands.

Brothel Parrot

A woman goes into a pet shop and decides to buy a parrot.

The assistant says, 'I must warn you: this parrot used to live in a brothel.' The woman is concerned, but decides to buy it anyway.

When the woman gets home, she leaves the parrot in the lounge and waits for the reaction from her family.

Her son comes into the room. The parrot says, 'Who's a pretty boy, then?'

The woman thinks, 'That's OK.'

Then her daughter walks in. The parrot says, 'Hello, sexy.'

The woman thinks, 'Well, that's not too bad. I shouldn't have worried.'

Then her husband gets back from work. The parrot says, 'Hi, John, not seen you since last week.'

BROWN AND HIDES

Q. What's brown and hides in the attic?
A. The diarrhoea of Anne Frank.

BULIMIC STAG DO

Q. How can you tell you're at a bulimic stag do?
A. The cake jumps out of the stripper.

BULLETS

A pregnant woman is walking down the street when she gets caught up in a bank robbery getaway and is shot three times in the stomach.

Miraculously, she makes a full recovery and gives birth to triplets: one boy and two girls.

One day, about 16 years later, one of the girls runs to the mother in tears.

The woman says, 'What's the matter?'

The daughter sobs, 'I went to the toilet and a bullet came out.'

A couple of weeks later, the second girl runs in crying, after exactly the same thing has happened to her.

Another week later, the boy runs to his mother and, like his sisters, he's in tears.

His mother says, 'Let me guess: you went to the toilet and a bullet came out?'

The boy says, 'No, I was having a wank and I shot the dog!'

BUMPKIN CIRCUMCISION

Q. How do you circumcise a bloke from Norwich?
A. Kick his sister in the jaw.

CANCER AND ALZHEIMER'S

Doctor: 'I have very bad news. You've got cancer and Alzheimer's.'

Patient: 'Well, at least I don't have cancer.'

CANNIBAL

Q. What did the cannibal do after he dumped his girlfriend?
A. Wiped his arse.

CARDBOARD BOX

Q. What's worse than a cardboard box?
A. Paper tits.

CAT GOES WOOF

Q. How do you make a cat go woof?
A. Cover it in petrol and light a match.

CAUGHT SPEEDING

What's the difference between getting caught speeding and going down on a woman?

When you go down on a woman, you can see the twat behind the bush.

CHEMIST AND CONDOMS

A girl asks her boyfriend to come over on Friday night and have dinner with her parents, and says that after dinner, she'd like to have sex with him for the first time.

The boy is ecstatic, but he's never had sex before, so he goes to the chemist to get some condoms.

The chemist asks the boy how many condoms he'd like to buy: a three-pack, a six-pack or a 10-pack. The boy chooses the 10-pack because he reckons he'll be busy.

That night, the boy shows up at the girl's house and meets his girlfriend at the door.

She says, 'Oh, I'm so excited that you're going to meet my parents. Come in!'

The boy goes inside and is taken to the dinner table, where the girl's parents are seated. The boy decides to say grace and bows his head.

Ten seconds passes, and the boy is still deep in prayer, with his head down.

Twenty seconds pass, and still no movement from the boy.

Finally, after the boy has spent a minute with his head down, his girlfriend leans over and whispers, 'I had no idea you were this religious.'

The boy whispers back, 'I had no idea your dad was a chemist.'

CLEVER MIDGET

Q. What is the difference between a clever midget and a venereal disease?
A. One is a cunning runt...

"Jim, you bonehead, you have your phaser set on ejaculate."

CLICK

Q. What goes, 'Click... Is that it? Click... Is that it? Click... Is that it?'
A. A blind person with a Rubik's cube.

CURE FOR AIDS

Q. Why haven't scientists found a cure for AIDS?
A. They can't get the laboratory mice to do anal.

DEODORANT

A man goes into a chemist and asks for some deodorant.
The assistant says, 'Ball or aerosol?'
The man says, 'Neither. It's for my armpits.'

DILDO AND SOY

Q. What do a dildo and soy beans have in common?
A. They're both used as meat substitutes.

DOCTOR'S GUILT

A doctor's just finished a marathon shagging session with a patient when he gets a tinge of guilt.
He thinks, 'It wasn't really ethical to screw one of my patients.'
But a little voice in his head says, 'Who cares? I bet lots of doctors do it.'
That makes the doctor feel a bit better, until another little voice says, 'But they probably aren't vets.'

DOG LICKS

Q. Why does a dog lick its penis?
A. Because it can't make a fist.

DUCK AND BREAD

A duck walks into a pub and says to the landlord, 'Got any bread?'

The landlord says, 'No.'

The duck says, 'Got any bread?'

The landlord says, 'No, we haven't got any bread.'

The duck says, 'Got any bread?'

The landlord says, 'No, we haven't got any bloody bread.'

The duck says, 'Got any bread?'

The landlord says, 'Are you deaf? Ask me for bread once more and I'll nail your fucking beak to the bar.'

The duck says, 'Got any nails?'

The landlord says, 'No.'

The duck says, 'Got any bread?'

DWARF

Q. What does a dwarf get when he runs through a woman's legs?
A. A clit round the ear and a flap across the face.

DYSLEXIC PIMP

Q. Did you hear about the dyslexic pimp?
A. He opened a warehouse.

WHY THE DINOSAURS DIED OUT

ELEPHANT AND CAMEL

An elephant says to a camel, 'Why are your boobs on your back?'

The camel says, 'That's rich, coming from someone with a dick on his face.'

EMOTIONS

A bloke holds a party where his guests are asked to dress as different emotions.

The first guest arrives. The host opens the door to see a

bloke covered in green paint with the letters 'N' and 'V' painted on his chest.

He says 'What emotion have you come as?'

The bloke says, 'I'm green with envy.'

A few minutes later, the next guest arrives. The host opens the door to see a woman covered in a pink body stocking with a feather boa wrapped around her privates.

The host says, 'What emotion are you?'

She says, 'I'm tickled pink.'

A couple of minutes later, the doorbell rings for the third time and the man opens the door to see two Irish blokes, Paddy and Mick, standing there stark naked, one with his cock in a bowl of custard and the other with his cock stuck in a pear.

Shocked, the host says, 'What emotions are these supposed to be?'

Paddy says, 'Well, I'm fucking discustard, and Mick has just come in despair.'

EROTIC AND KINKY

Q. What's the difference between erotic and kinky?

A. Erotic is using a feather; kinky is using the whole chicken.

FANCY DRESS

A bloke goes to a fancy dress party dressed only in his Y-fronts.

The host says, 'What are you supposed to be?'

The bloke says, 'Premature ejaculation: I've just come in my pants.'

FIRST SIGN

Q. What's the first sign of AIDS?

A. A pounding sensation in the arse.

Fathers' jobs

The teacher says, 'Let's discuss what your dads do for a living.'

Mary says, 'My dad is a lawyer; He puts bad guys in jail.'

Jack says, 'My dad is a doctor; He makes sick people better.'

Johnny doesn't raise his hand, so the teacher says, 'Johnny, what does your dad do?'

Johnny says, 'My dad's dead.'

The teacher says, 'I'm sorry to hear that. But what did he do before he died?'

Johnny says, 'He turned blue and shat on the carpet.'

GAY ROW

Did you hear about the two gay blokes who had a row in a pub?
  They went outside to exchange blows.

GAY THEME PARK

Q. How can you tell you're in a gay theme park?
A. They issue gerbils at the Tunnel of Love.

GAY WESTERN

Q. How can you tell if a Western is gay?
A. All the good guys are hung.

GREEN AND YELLOW

Q. What's green and yellow and eats nuts?
A. Gonorrhoea.

GREY RIDDLE

Q. What's grey, sits at the end of your bed and takes the piss?
A. A kidney dialysis machine.

G-SPOT AND GOLF BALL

Q. What's the difference between a G-spot and a golf ball?
A. A man will actually search for a golf ball.

GYNO AND PUPPY

Q. What do a short-sighted gynaecologist and a puppy have in common?
A. A wet nose.

GYPSY

Q. What's the best thing about fingering a gypsy during her period?
A. You get your palm red for free.

HORMONE

Q. How do you make a hormone?
A. Don't pay her.

IN THE ARMY

Q. Why is being in the army like a blow-job?
A. The closer you get to discharge, the better you feel.

IRISHMAN FALLS FLAT

An Irishman has been drinking at a pub all night.

The landlord finally says that the bar is closing. But when the Irishman stands up to leave, he falls flat on his face. He tries to stand again, with the same result.

He decides to crawl outside and get some fresh air to sober him up.

Once outside, he tries to stand up – but again falls flat on his face. So he decides to crawl home. When he arrives at the door, he tries to stand up – but again falls flat on his face. He crawls through the door and into his bedroom.

When he reaches his bed, he tries once again to stand up. This time he manages to pull himself upright, but immediately he collapses on to the duvet and falls asleep.

He's awakened the next morning by his wife shouting, 'So, you've been out drinking again!'

He says, 'What makes you say that?'

She says, 'The pub called – you left your wheelchair there again.'

JACK THE RIPPER

Q. What's worse than getting raped by Jack the Ripper?
A. Getting fingered by Captain Hook.

KILTS

Q. Why do Scotsmen wear kilts?
A. Because the sheep can hear a zip a mile away.

LABOUR PAINS

A woman goes into labour.

After hours of struggle, the baby pops out. The doctor, looking worried, picks it up and rushes it to intensive care.

The parents get more and more concerned as the hours pass, until finally the doctor returns.

He says, 'There's good news and bad news. The bad news is, your baby's ginger.'

The mother says, 'What's the good news?'

The doctor says, 'It's dead.'

LEGS

Q. What has two grey legs and two brown legs?
A. An elephant with diarrhoea.

LESBIAN PERIODS

Q. What do you call two lesbians on their period?
A. Finger painting.

LESBIAN VIAGRA

Q. What do lesbians use as Viagra?
A. Batteries.

LUMBER TRUCK

Q. Why did the lumber truck stop?
A. To let the lumber jack off.

MEDICAL SCHOOL

First-year students at medical school are receiving their first
anatomy class with a dead human body.

They gather around the surgery table with the body covered
by a white sheet.

The professor says, 'In medicine, you need two qualities. The
first is that you must not be disgusted by anything involving
the human body.'

As an example, the professor pulls back the sheet, sticks his
finger in the arse of the corpse, withdraws it and sticks his
finger in his mouth.

'Go ahead and do the same thing,' he says.

The students hesitate, but eventually take turns sticking a finger in the arse of the dead body and then sucking on it.

When everyone has finished, the Professor says, 'The second most important quality is observation. I stuck in my middle finger and sucked on my index finger. Now learn to pay attention...'

MONKEY AND CHAINSAW

Q. How is a monkey like a chainsaw?
A. They both fuck up trees.

MORE BRAINS

Q. Why do women have two per cent more brains than a cow?
A. So that when you pull their tits they won't shit on the floor.

"I'm afraid it's the only style I know."

MOUNT OLIVE

Q. What happened when Jesus went to Mount Olive?
A. Popeye kicked the crap out of him.

NEVER BEEN KISSED

A man is walking on the beach when he sees a woman with no arms and legs lying by the shore crying.

He says, 'What's the matter?'

She says, 'I've never been kissed.'

So he kneels down and gives her a peck on the lips.

The woman smiles and the man starts to walk away, but after a few steps he hears her crying again.

So he goes back and says, 'What's the matter?'

She says, 'I've never been screwed.'

So the man picks the woman up, throws her in the sea and shouts, 'You're screwed now!'

NEW EXORCIST

Did you hear about the new Exorcist film?

They get the Devil to come in to take the priest out of the child.

NEW TAMPONS

Have you heard about the new line of tampons that have bells and tinsel?

It's for the Christmas period.

NUNS AND DRACULA

Two nuns are driving along a country lane at midnight when Dracula jumps on their bonnet.

The first nun says, 'Show him your cross!'

So the second nun shakes her fist and yells, 'Get off my fucking car!'

NUNS' SCANDAL

Three nuns are talking.

The first nun says, 'I was cleaning in Father Hilton's room the other day and do you know what I found? A bunch of pornographic magazines.'

The second nun says, 'What did you do?'

The first nun says, 'I threw them in the bin.'

The second nun says, 'I can top that. I was in Father Hilton's room putting away the laundry and I found a bunch of condoms.'

The first nun says, 'What did you do?'

The second nun says, 'I poked holes in all of them.'

The third nun faints.

ONLY ANIMAL

Q. What's the only animal with an arsehole in the middle of its back?

A. A police horse.

OXYGEN MASK

A man is lying in hospital with an oxygen mask over his mouth and nose, and is still heavily sedated from a four-hour operation.

A young nurse appears to sponge his hands and feet.

'Nurse,' the man mumbles from behind the mask, 'are my testicles black?'

Embarrassed, the young nurse says, 'I don't know; I'm only here to wash your hands and feet.'

He struggles again to ask, 'Nurse, are my testicles black?'

So she pulls back the sheets, raises his gown, holds his penis in one hand and his testicles in her other hand, takes a close look and says, 'There's nothing wrong with them!'

The man pulls off his oxygen mask and says very slowly, 'That felt great – but are... my... test... results... back?'

MALCOLM REALISED YORKSHIRE LADYBOYS WEREN'T AS EXOTIC AS THE THAI VERSION

PAEDOPHILES ON A BEACH

Two paedophiles are on a beach.
   One says to the other, 'Can you get out of my son, please?'

PAEDOPHILES ON A BENCH

Two paedophiles are sitting on a park bench when an 11-year-old girl walks past.
   One says to the other, 'She used to be a right goer in her day.'

PIES

Q. What's the difference between pussy and apple pie?
A. You can eat your mum's apple pie.

POP SVENGALI AND GYNO

What's the difference between a pop Svengali and a gynaecologist?
   A pop Svengali fucks his singers and a gynaecologist sucks his fingers.

PURPLE AND PINK

Q. What's the difference between purple and pink?
A. The grip.

ROOSTER AND FLEA

Q. What do you get when you cross a rooster with a flea?
A. An itchy cock.

SERIOUSLY ILL

A woman is seriously ill, so her husband takes her to the doctor.
   The doctor says, 'It's either Alzheimer's or AIDS.'
   The husband says, 'How do we find out which?'
   The doctor says, 'Go for a long drive in the countryside, have a picnic, then leave her in the field. If she gets home, don't fuck her.'

SKUNKS

Q. What do you call two skunks in the 69 position?
A. Odour eaters.

SNOOKER PLAYER

Q. Why did the snooker player go to the toilet?
A. To pot the brown.

SOFT AND WARM

Q. What's soft and warm when you go to bed, but hard and stiff when you wake up?
A. Vomit.

Special Watch

An arrogant man walks into a wine bar and takes a seat next to an attractive woman.

He gives her a quick glance, then casually looks at his watch.

The woman notices this and says, 'Is your girlfriend running late?'

He says, 'No, I just brought this state-of-the-art watch and I was testing it.'

Intrigued, the woman says, 'A state-of-the-art watch? What's so special about it?'

He says, 'It uses alpha waves to talk to me telepathically.'

She says, 'What's it telling you now?'

He says, 'It says you're not wearing any knickers.'

The woman says, 'Well, it must be broken, because actually I am wearing knickers.'

The man says, 'Bloody thing; must be an hour fast.'

SPERM CANCELLATION

Q. What's the best way to cancel an appointment at the sperm bank?
A. Phone up and say you can't come.

SPERM RECEPTION

Q. What does the receptionist at the sperm clinic say to clients as they're leaving?
A. 'Thanks for coming.'

STARTS WITH A P

Q. What always starts with a p?
A. A shit.

STUCK TO THE FLOOR

A woman's having a shower when she slips over on the bathroom floor.

But instead of falling forwards or backwards, she slips sideways, does the splits and suctions herself to the floor.

She yells and her husband comes running.

She says, 'I've suctioned myself to the floor!'

He tries to pull her up, but can't.

He says, 'You're just too heavy. I'll go across the road and get a mate to help.'

He comes back with a mate, but, hard as they pull, they still can't get her off the floor.

The mate says, 'I've got an idea.'

His husband says, 'What's that?'

The mate says, 'I'll go home and get my hammer and chisel and we'll break the tiles under her.'

The husband says, 'OK. While you're doing that, I'll stay here and play with her tits.'

The mate says, 'Play with her tits? Why?'

The husband says, 'Well, if I can get her wet enough, we can slide her into the kitchen where the tiles aren't so expensive.'

SUBSTITUTE PRIEST

A priest has been in the confessional all day without a break.

He's desperate to take a dump, but people keep coming to confess and he hates to leave.

Eventually, he peers out of his cubicle and signals the janitor to come over. He asks the janitor to cover for him, gives him the confessions book, then rushes off in the direction of the toilet.

The janitor is bewildered, but he goes into the confessional and sits down.

A woman on the other side says, 'Bless me, Father, for I have sinned. I cheated on my husband.'

The janitor scans through the book until he finds 'Adultery'. He tells the woman to say 50 Hail Marys and wash in holy water.

Next comes a man who says, 'Bless me, Father, for I have sinned. I had oral sex with another man.'

The janitor hunts through the book, but he can't find a penance for oral sex.

He leans out of the confessional and whispers to an altar-boy, 'What does the priest give for oral sex?'

The boy says, 'Five quid and a chocolate bar.'

TALKING CLOCK

After a night out, a man brings his mates back to show off his new house.

The visitors are perplexed by a large gong in the lounge.

One says, 'What's that big brass gong for?'

The host says, 'That's my Talking Clock.'

The guest says, 'How does it work?'

The host says, 'I'll show you', and gives the gong an ear-shattering blow with an unpadded hammer.

A woman's voice from upstairs screams, 'For fuck's sake, it's twenty to two in the fucking morning!'

TEST TUBE BABY

Q. What's the worst thing about being a test tube baby?
A. You know for sure that your dad's a wanker.

THREE OLD LADIES

Three old ladies are walking down the street when a man in a dirty raincoat appears and flashes them.

Two have a stroke; one can't reach.

TORTOISE

A tortoise gets raped by two snails.

'Describe them,' says the policeman.

'I can't,' says the tortoise, 'it all happened so fast.'

TWO CONDOMS

Two condoms walk past a gay bar.

One turns to the other and says, 'Fancy going in there and getting shit-faced?'

TYRES

Q. What's the difference between a rubber tyre and 365 blow-jobs?
A. One is a Goodyear, the other is a great year.

UGLIEST CHILDREN

Q. What sexual position produces the ugliest children?
A. Ask your mum.

Tough Prostitute

A hard bloke walks into a brothel holding two unopened bottles of beer and growls, 'I'm looking for the roughest, toughest prostitute in town.'

The pimp says, 'No problem. She's upstairs, second room on the right.'

The hard bloke stomps up the stairs, kicks the door open and bellows, 'I'm looking for the roughest, toughest prostitute in town.'

The woman inside the room says, 'You found her!'

She strips naked, bends over and grabs her ankles.

The hard man says, 'How do you know I want that position first?'

The prostitute says, 'I don't. I just thought you might want to open those beers first.'

VAMPIRE

A vampire goes into a pub and asks for some boiling water.
   The landlord says, 'I thought you only drank blood?'
   The vampire pulls out a used tampon and says, 'I'm making tea.'

VET AND DOG

Q. What did the vet say to the dog who kept licking his balls?
A. 'Thanks!'

WAITER'S HORROR

A waiter is walking around his restaurant when he notices three men at the door masturbating.
   He says, 'What the hell are you doing?'
   The first bloke says, 'We saw the notice on your wall saying, "First come, first served."'

WASHING MACHINE

Q. Why does your washing machine laugh?
A. It's taking the piss out of your pants.

WELSHMAN'S ANIMALS

Q. What do you call a Welshman who owns goats as well as sheep?
A. Bisexual.

WELSHMAN'S SHEEP

Q. What do you call a Welshman with a sheep under each arm?
A. A pimp.

WOMEN IN A BAR

Three women are in a bar.

The first says, 'I've had sex so many times I can fit four fingers up my vagina.'

The second says, 'Well, I can fit my whole arm up.'

The third women says nothing, while slowly sliding down over her bar stool.

WOMEN IN HEAVEN

Q. Why do only ten per cent of women go to heaven?
A. Because if they all went, it would be hell.

ZEBRA

Q. What is a zebra?
A. Twenty-five sizes larger than an 'A' bra.